Economic and Social Commission for Asia and the Pacific

Asian Population Studies Series No. 160

# Migration Patterns and Policies
# in the Asian and Pacific Region

# United Nations
## New York, 2003

ST/ESCAP/2277

| UNITED NATIONS PUBLICATION |
|---|
| Sales No. E.03.II.F.56 |
| Copyright © United Nations 2003 |
| ISBN: 92-1-120330-9 |

# PREFACE

The Economic and Social Commission for Asia and the Pacific organized the Ad Hoc Expert Group Meeting on Migration and Development: Opportunities and Challenges for Poverty Reduction in the ESCAP Region at Bangkok from 28 to 30 November 2001. The Meeting was a part of the preparatory activities for the Fifth Asian and Pacific Population Conference, held at Bangkok in December 2002. The main purposes of the Meeting were to:

♦ Review migration trends and patterns in the region, with a focus on international migration, and their implications for poverty reduction;

♦ Examine the policies and programmes on migration that have been adopted in the various countries;

♦ Make specific recommendations to better understand and manage migration flows and contribute to the well-being of individual migrants and society as a whole.

The Meeting was attended by a number of senior officials and experts from selected countries of the region. The present study is based on background papers presented at the Meeting. It is hoped that the results of this study will be useful for planners, policy makers and researchers.

# SUMMARY

Migration has become an important social phenomenon in Asia. Patterns of migration have been firmly established in the region. In chapter I Battistella makes several key observations about migration trends in Asia. In the area of labour migration, there has been an increase of 44 per cent in annual movement since 1990, involving at least 2 million workers. A complex system of labour recruitment has been entrenched in almost all Asian countries, emphasizing the crucial role of mediators in the migration process. In addition, labour migration has been characterized by an increasing proportion of women.

Unauthorized migration forms a significant component of migration flows in the region and is a result of migration policies that fail to reflect the interplay between the demand for migrant labour and migration pressure. The author emphasizes the need to address the problem of smuggling migrants and human trafficking, especially women and children. He notes that unauthorized migration is a response to structural deficiency in the migration process in Asia – for example, policies to tackle illegal migration are usually unilateral, and therefore less effective than they would be if bilateral or regional.

The author also examines a link between migration and poverty. While poverty creates the aspiration to migrate, it does not itself lead one to the decision to migrate. Moreover, it is not the poorest who migrate but those with some degree of financial and human capital. It has been shown that remittances contribute substantially to the economies of the countries of origin, and hence help to alleviate poverty. The author concludes that the volume, direction and composition of migration flows in Asia will continue to be shaped by economic and political factors.

The huge disparities in economic development and welfare between the island States of the South Pacific are key factors driving international migration in the region, which has occurred since the 1960s. In chapter II Connell examines how migration is affected by socio-economic needs and demographic changes in the region. He studies recent migration trends in the three major indigenous groups – Polynesia, Micronesia, Melanesia – in particular, the issue of internal migration and urbanization.

It has been observed that prospects for economic growth in the tiny island States of the South Pacific are highly limited. This is primarily due to the inherent disadvantages of being small, and partly explains why the Pacific islands are the most heavily aid-assisted countries in the world. International migration has played a crucial role in relieving the burden of Governments in providing employment and welfare services to a growing population, hence aiding the effectiveness of national development efforts in the short run.

Some States in the region are facing the problem of "brain drain" as countries worldwide seek the skills of the talented and educated. The Pacific is also experiencing the widespread phenomenon of urbanization as people move to the cities in search of jobs and better living conditions. Growing inequalities, real or perceived, and rising expectations have deepened the aspirations to migrate. This has created a myriad of problems, one of which is increased hostility and suspicion towards such migrants, who are often perceived to be the cause of rising urban crime rates and other developmental problems.

In this chapter the author also examines the linkage between migration, poverty and development. He notes that urban poverty is on the rise and that migration has transferred rural poverty to urban areas. Indeed growing unemployment and the proliferation of informal employment in the forms of prostitution, begging and crime will present a major challenge to governance and urban planning in the Pacific. On the whole, the growth and development of the Pacific islands are increasingly challenged by a globalized economic system. The author concludes that there is a pressing need for Governments in the region to create employment for rising populations with higher expectations; cope with international fluctuations in demand, trade and economic growth; restructure and diversify domestic economics; and gain international economic competitiveness.

In chapter III Wongboonsin examines current migration policies in the Asian and Pacific region, identifying similarities and disparities among the highly diverse countries in the region. She focuses on international migration as well as studies national policies from the perspectives of both sending and receiving countries. International migration has become more complex in the Asian and Pacific region today owing to the changing demographic and social developmental patterns in many countries and the rise of cross-border movement of both documented and undocumented migrants, according to the author. Governments in this region have identified international migration as an important area for policy considerations as migrants not only affect the economic growth of the countries involved but also have consequential implications for political and social change.

It is generally observed that there has been a trend towards a tightening of immigration rules with regard to cheap and low-end foreign workers. On the other hand, countries continue to open their doors to highly skilled and high-end foreign workers, in recognition of their potential contribution to a society's progress towards a knowledge economy. Bilateral agreements between receiving and sending countries are becoming a useful strategy to achieve the double benefits of minimizing risks and maximizing national economic growth at the same time.

Governments in the region continue to view undocumented migrants with suspicion and disdain, and have tightened their border controls and imposed stiffer penalties in order to restrict the inflow of such migrants. The author concludes that the problem of human smuggling and trafficking in the region remains a major challenge and, together with the issues of forced migration and of remittances as a tool in economic development, will demand greater regional cooperation so as to produce orderly migration that advances national development.

# CONTENTS

# CHAPTER I

# INTERNATIONAL MIGRATION IN ASIA

By Graziano Battistella[*]

International migration in East, South-East and South Asia at the beginning of the new millennium presents a complex typology. Perhaps the best way to convey the idea of complexity is by quoting some recent newspaper headlines, all dated 5 November 2002: "700,000 foreigners in sectors shunned by locals" was an item in the *New Straits Times* in Kuala Lumpur. "Returnees tricked into signing forms", stated the *Bangkok Post* in referring to the repatriation of 63 people to Myanmar. In reference to the Republic of Korea, the *Kyodo News Service* stated: "Japan to ease visa restrictions". *The Financial Times* reported: "Smugglers see Afghans as potential prey". From a few newspaper headlines on a day chosen at random, one may observe the gamut of the various migration flows of concern in Asia: labour migrants, immigrants, unauthorized migrants and potential asylum seekers. Missing were articles on the migration of highly skilled people, because that is a type of migration which does not often make newspaper headlines.

The variety of headlines also conveys the idea that migration has become an important social phenomenon in Asia. Its importance refers not only to the number of people involved, but also to the implications for societies and economies in the countries concerned. What was said about migration in general, that "political decisions about international migration will be among the most important made over the next two decades" (Massey and others, 1998, p. 58), is certainly applicable to Asia. However, international forums of Asian policy makers treat migration with benign neglect. Among the reasons for such neglect is the stabilization of migration patterns over the previous 30 years, ensuring some level of predictability as migration most probably will not change drastically in the near future.

[*] Scalabrini International Migration Institute, Rome, Italy.

One of the main points of this paper is that migration flows in the region have found their course and will tend to maintain it. Even major events might not modify those trends profoundly. The financial crisis of 1997/98, for instance, had a limited, mostly temporary impact on migration flows. The recovery from the crisis restored the flows to their established course, with some adjustments. This point will emerge in the descriptive section of the paper, and it includes unauthorized migration, which constitutes a relevant portion of migration in the region. Its pervasiveness seriously questions its representation as an anomaly in a social phenomenon defined by control and restrictions. At the same time, and this is the second point, migration is not insensitive to economic and political conditions developing in the region. In particular, we will try to speculate how migration might develop in the region in light of the current international recession. A final section is dedicated to the linkage between migration and poverty, and provides a few final considerations.

## THEORETICAL NOTE

Before moving to the description of flows and trends, it is necessary to provide a short theoretical note as the premise for helping to orient the discussion. Researchers on migration have expressed their dissatisfaction over the past two decades with a theoretical approach prevalent all this time. That approach was based on the idea that migrants are rational people who make rational choices and that migration decisions are based mostly on responses to wage differentials (real or expected) between countries. Presented in different terms, such an approach emphasizes the so-called push and pull factors, and examines the intervening obstacles to explain why people move. The movement of people will cease when differentials diminish, and as conditions at the points of origin and destination tend towards equilibrium. The longevity of such an approach rests on the immediate understanding of the dynamics of migration that it provides. However, critics have emphasized that the model leaves too many aspects unexplained. In particular, it does not explain why there is so little migration from countries that present all conditions for migration, why some people who share the same conditions as migrants do not go abroad, why migration takes certain directions and not others, and why migration persists beyond the time when it is very advantageous.

New models have surfaced in recent years, bringing additional understanding to the dynamics of migration. Without going into a detailed description of such models,[1] it is relevant to point to some conclusions derived from them. Among such conclusions are the following:

(a) Attention should be given to the fact that migration is not just an individual choice, but a choice taking place within a household, which intends to minimize the risks of various markets (crop, capital, credit, insurance) and to improve its conditions in relation to other households.

(b) Labour markets tend towards segmentation, where entry-level workers leave their jobs with low social prestige, creating a scarcity of labour that employers offset by importing migrants. As migration is generated by the demand of employers for workers, with the mediation of labour recruiters, migrant wages do not respond to market conditions and are kept low through institutional mechanisms.

(c) International labour flows do not occur randomly, but respond to linkages established through history (colonialism) and economic interaction. Investments from capitalist (core) countries initiate a type of development in developing (periphery) countries which causes displacement and migration in the opposite direction of investments.

(d) The costs involved in international migration, deriving from a lack of capital and lack of information, are offset by social networks that facilitate the movement of people who can enter into such networks and ensure the continuation of migration beyond the attractiveness of differentials.

(e) Migration is not neutral; it brings about changes both in the societies of origin (where a culture of migration tends to form) and that of destination (where migrants tend to occupy niches in the labour market which can be accessed only by other migrants). The cumulative changes brought about by migration ensure that migration flows will continue beyond the original intentions.

It appears consequential that the various insights deriving from the new theoretical approaches to migration will suggest different strategies to Governments that intend to manage migration rather than simply affect wages. In fact, as policies become more restrictive and migration pressures increase, "the most important forces operating to influence the volume and composition of international migration today are those that States deploy to regulate or impede the inflow" (Massey and others, 1998, p. 14).

---

[1] For a detailed discussion of this issue, see Massey and others, 1998, from which the following notes are taken.

It has also become apparent that no single model is sufficient to explain international migration. In this paper, which is of a general descriptive nature, it is maintained that at the basis of migration movements in Asia are demographic, social, economic and political disparities among countries. However, such disparities did not and do not automatically generate migration. Rather, migrations have been triggered by colonial ties, displacements caused by foreign investments, the demand for labour in the segmented labour markets of fast-developing economies, and the need to seek alternative solutions for households facing non-performing agricultural, capital, credit and insurance markets. Once established, the migratory flows have been sustained by relative deprivation, social networks and the recruitment industry. Policies have played a significant role in determining the size and composition of migration flows. How policies will change with the modification of the basic disparities will determine the development of various migrations in Asia.

## MIGRATION TRENDS IN ASIA

The various subregions of Asia have been characterized by specific migratory movements. Traditionally, South Asia is identified as a subregion of origin of migration, East Asia as a subregion of destination and South-East Asia as a subregion of both origin and destination. Such a characterization maintains its validity as the issue of migration can then be inserted into the larger social and political discourse of the various subregions. At the same time, however, migration flows have developed in different directions, particularly within the various regions, so that it is difficult to maintain the traditional characterizations. In East Asia, for instance, migration from China, although unauthorized, has become important in Japan and the Republic of Korea, and Koreans continue to enter Japan. South Asia cannot be considered just a subregion of origin, in view of the substantial migration from Bangladesh and Nepal to India. The recent project to include China and the Association of South-East Asian Nations (ASEAN) in one free trade area, although still 10 years away, hints of possible consequences for human mobility and the blurring of regional distinctions. This paper, therefore, describes migration flows by their characteristics, rather than separately by geographic subregion. Nonetheless, geographic areas remain useful for a general description of size and directions of flows.

### Labour migration

The first characteristic is the diversification of direction and composition of flows determined, to some extent, by migration policies. The origin of overseas

4

work from Asia is traditionally set at the beginning of the 1970s, when workers from India and Pakistan were hired for the booming construction projects in the Persian Gulf countries. They were later joined by the Philippines and then Bangladesh, Indonesia and Sri Lanka. During the previous 30 years, the flow of migrant labour towards Western Asia (sometimes referred to as the Middle East) went through some important changes: first, it expanded from occupations related to the construction of facilities and infrastructure to occupations related to maintenance and services; second, it became more diversified in its gender composition, with the increasing presence of women among the migrants; third, it witnessed a progressive decline in wages, as competition among countries of origin and migrant recruiters led to acceptance of lower conditions; finally, this flow met official opposition from the Persian Gulf countries, trying to substitute migrant labour with local workers.

Declining opportunities in Western Asia, sometimes because of force majeure, as in the case of the Persian Gulf war in 1991 and increasing opportunities in East and South-East Asia, led migrant labour flows to take new routes. Singapore has adopted a pragmatic approach to migrant labour since the early 1970s, periodically adjusting its measures to respond to the demands of a fast-growing economy. Originally limited to workers from Malaysia, employers in Singapore were allowed in 1978 to hire migrants from Bangladesh, India, Indonesia, the Philippines, Sri Lanka and Thailand and in 1984 from what is now Hong Kong, China; Macao, China; the Republic of Korea; and Taiwan Province of China (Wong, 1997). Expansion led to the current situation of approximately 560,000 workers being employed in Singapore. Facing the need to control the influx of Chinese from the mainland (150 a day), Hong Kong, China looked for migrant workers from other countries, mostly for specific projects. At the same time, it allowed the hiring of foreign workers in the domestic sector, opportunities seized mostly by the Philippines (136,000) and more recently by Indonesia (54,000) and Thailand (27,000).

The opposition of Japan and the Republic of Korea to the import of migrant labour should have kept migrant workers out of those countries. However, labour demands were met in different ways. Japan utilized workers of Japanese descent from Brazil (254,394 in 2000) and Peru (46,171) (*Migration News*, November 2001) and established a training programme where trainees also functioned as workers. The Republic of Korea also had recourse to training; however, the high demand for foreign labour inadequately met by trainees led to a spillover from training to unauthorized migration. As of August 2000, of 267,627 foreign workers, trainees comprised 29.5 per cent and unauthorized migrants 65.6 per cent

(Choi, 2001). A recent proposal by that country's Labour Ministry would reduce training to one year and then allow trainees to stay for two years as migrant workers (*Asian Migration News*, 31 August 2001).

In contrast to Japan and the Republic of Korea, Taiwan Province of China adopted a policy of admitting migrant labour only from Indonesia, Malaysia (which practically did not make use of it), the Philippines and Thailand and recently Viet Nam. In about 10 years, the number of foreign workers reached 326,261 at the end of August 2001. Typically, workers are employed in three sectors: manufacturing, construction and services.

At the opposite end of the spectrum one could locate the labour flows to Malaysia and Thailand, which developed initially without much policy involvement and were later regulated through measures designed to allow the maximum flexibility for the economy to use or discard foreign labour. Proximity to countries of origin with a large supply of labour, lax implementation of border controls and an active middleman system resulted in these two countries hosting the largest number of migrants among Asian countries, although a large proportion of them were unauthorized workers (tables 1 and 2).

A similar situation has developed in India. Easily accessible Nepalese workers have found employment in India, but their actual number varies from a low of 250,000, according to government estimates, to approximately 3 million as estimated by the All India Migrant Nepali Association (Prasad, 2000). Along the eastern side of the Indian border, perhaps 500,000 Bangladeshis may have moved to Assam State since 1971, increasing the incidence of ethnic strife with the local population. Policies concerning this issue are unclear.

This brief overview of labour migration flows in parts of the subregions points to the decisive role played by migration policies. A similarly important role is played by the mediators in the migration process. In practically all Asian countries, a system of labour recruitment has prospered, with rather similar characteristics. Agents are normally licensed by the Government to operate for the purpose of facilitating the placement of workers abroad and expanding employment opportunities in the country of origin. For their services, agents, who originally had been paid by the employers for the procurement of labour, eventually were allowed to charge workers a regulated, but oftentimes violated, placement fee. Not all countries have adopted a standard labour contract, diversified by occupation and country of destination. However, even in countries and areas with such standards, the practice is often disregarded because of

6

## Table 1. Stock of authorized Asian migrants in selected countries and areas of Asia

| From / To | Indonesia | Philippines | Thailand | China | Bangladesh | Myanmar | Other | Total migrants[a] | Most recent total[b] |
|---|---|---|---|---|---|---|---|---|---|
| Japan[c] | 11 936 | 93 265 | 20 669 | 252 164 | 5 900 | | 1 098 773 | 1 482 707 | 1 448 000 |
| Republic of Korea[d] | 9 600 | 10 800 | 26 700 | | 6 300 | | 95 300 | 148 700 | 298 400 |
| Taiwan Province of China[e] | 77 830 | 98 161 | 142 665 | | | | 7 859 | 326 515 | 326 515 |
| Hong Kong, China[f] | 34 300 | 146 400 | 25 000 | | | | | 205 700 | 215 000 |
| Thailand | | | | | | 132 800 | 27 200 | 160 000 | 160 000 |
| Malaysia[g] | 517 766 | 30 510 | 2 888 | | 129 004 | | 22 054 | 702 222 | 732 588 |
| Singapore[h] | 100 000 | 60 000 | 60 000 | 46 000 | | | 184 000 | 450 000 | 580 000 |

*Sources*: **Japan:** Susumu Watanabe (1998). "The economic crisis and migrant workers in Japan", *Asian and Pacific Migration Journal*, vol. 7, Nos. 2-3. **Republic of Korea:** Organisation for Economic Co-operation and Development (OECD) SOPEMI (1998). *Trends in International Migration: Annual Report*, (Paris, OECD).

**Taiwan Province of China:** Central Intelligence Agency (CIA) (2000). *The World Factbook 2000*, <http://www.odci.gov/cia/publications/factbook/index.html>

**Hong Kong, China:** Sek-hong Ng and Grace O.M. Lee (1998). "Hong Kong labor market in the aftermath of the crisis: Implications for foreign workers", *Asian and Pacific Migration Journal*, vol. 7, Nos. 2-3, pp. 171-186.

**Thailand:** Scalabrini Migration Center estimates based on Joseph Dawes (2001). "Beware the alien invasion", *Asiaweek*, 14 September.

**Malaysia:** Graziano Battistella (2001). "Migration 2000 in Asia: A year in review", *Asian Migration*, vol. 14, No. 1.

**Singapore:** International Labour Organization (ILO) (1998). "The social impact of the Asian financial crisis", technical report for discussion at the High-Level Tripartite Meeting on Social Responses to the Financial Crisis in East and South-East Asian Countries, Bangkok, 22-24 April 1998, Bangkok, ILO Regional Office for Asia and the Pacific).

[a] Include also non-Asians.
[b] Based on Dawes (2001) above.
[c] For 1997, "other" includes 645,373 Koreans.
[d] For 1996.
[e] For end of 2000.
[f] For mid-1997.
[g] For February 2000.
[h] For 1998.

## Table 2 . Estimate of unauthorized migrants in selected Asian countries and areas

| From \ To | Japan[a] | Republic of Korea[c] | Taiwan Province of China[d] | Malaysia[e] | Singapore | Thailand[h] |
|---|---|---|---|---|---|---|
| Bangladesh | 5 864 | 13 774 | | 246 400 | | |
| Myanmar | 5 957 | | | 25 600 | | 484 926 |
| Cambodia | | | | | | 48 432 |
| China | 38 957 | 85 429 | | | | |
| Indonesia | | | 2 700 | 475 200 | | |
| Republic of Korea | 52 854 | | | | | |
| Malaysia | 10 926 | | 400 | | | |
| Mongolia | | 12 155 | | | | |
| Pakistan | 4 766 | 5 589 | | 12 000 | | |
| Philippines | 42 627 | 11 850 | 5 150 | 9 600[f] | | |
| Taiwan Province of China | 9 403 | | | | | |
| Thailand | 38 191 | 11 309 | 6 000 | 8 000 | | |
| Viet Nam | | 6 991 | | | | |
| Others | 72 242 | 25 404 | 5 750 | 23 200 | | 64 577 |
| Total | 281 787 | 172 501 | 20 000 | 800 000 | | 597 935 |
| Recent Total | 251 697[b] | 220 000[b] | | 600 000[b] | 350 000[g] | 1 000 000[b] |

*Sources:* **Japan:** Susumu Watanabe (1998). "The economic crisis and migrant workers in Japan", *Asian and Pacific Migration Journal,* vol. 7, Nos. 2-3.

**Republic of Korea:** Jin Ho Choi (2001). "International migration, human resource development and migration policy in Korea", *Asian and Pacific Migration Journal,* vol. 10, Nos. 3-4, pp. 463-484.

**Taiwan Province of China:** Joseph Lee (1998). "The impact of Asian financial crisis on foreign workers in Taiwan", *Asian and Pacific Migration Journal,* vol. 7, Nos. 2-3, pp. 145-170.

**Malaysia:** Azizah Kassim (1998). "The case of new receiving countries in the developing world: Malaysia", paper presented at the Technical Symposium on International Migration and Development, The Hague, 29 June-3 July.

**Thailand:** Thai Government estimate.

[a] Overstayers, end of 1997.

[b] *Asian Migration News* (2001). *<http://www.scalabrini.org/~smc/amnews/amnews.htm>,* 31 August.

[c] For 2000.

[d] Estimate based on overstayers and apprehensions.

[e] Estimate based on 1996 regularization.

[f] Add approximately 70,000 Filipinos still irregular in Sabah.

[g] Joseph Dawes (2001). "Beware the alien invasion", *Asiaweek,* 14 September.

[h] For end of 1998.

8

worsening labour conditions. In some countries, recruiters are held responsible for what might occur to the migrant during employment. The role of recruiters and that of other mediators, such as brokers in countries of destination as well as travel agents and government officials, is especially relevant not only for the expansion of migration flows, but also for the orderly development of overseas labour.

In addition to the direction of flows in response to migration policies and the activities of migration agents, labour migration in Asia is characterized by an increasing proportion of women. They dominate in migration flows from some countries such as the Philippines. In 1992, women accounted for 52 per cent of the newly hired Filipino overseas workers; in 2000, women comprised 70 per cent of the migrants. The share of women is very high also for migrants from Sri Lanka (65 per cent in 1999) (Scalabrini Migration Center, 2001) and those from Indonesia who go to Western Asia. The situation is different in other countries of origin, such as Bangladesh and Pakistan, where women are practically forbidden or discouraged from going abroad. The high percentage of women in migration is a direct consequence of the selection of industries that hire migrant workers and the traditional occupation of male or female labour in such industries. The service sector has become particularly relevant, specifically in the form of domestic services in Hong Kong, China; Malaysia; Singapore; and Taiwan Province of China, but also in Western Asia. In the United Arab Emirates, there are two house-helpers per household on average; in Singapore, 38 out of 50 surveyed families declared they could not survive a month without a domestic worker (Battistella, 2001). The health sector is also very important, with increasing demand for nurses and caregivers, particularly in Taiwan Province of China. Finally, the demand for employment in the entertainment industry, specifically in Japan, continues to account for 20 per cent of female migration from the Philippines, and a significant proportion from Thailand (most of it unauthorized). The large-scale employment of migrant women in some occupations of the service sector indicates that the feminization of migration is practically an irreversible trend.

Based on trends in the region, it can be said that labour migration has become structural in Asian countries. In addition to Western Asia, where most of the labour force in the private sector is foreign – 35 per cent in Saudi Arabia, 68 per cent in Kuwait and 75 per cent in the United Arab Emirates (Central Intelligence Agency, 2000) – migrants form 25 per cent of the labour force in Singapore and 16 per cent in Malaysia (Hui, 1998). The proportion is much lower (3 per cent) in Taiwan Province of China and Thailand, and even lower in Japan and the Republic of Korea. Nevertheless, the difficulty of these countries and areas in lowering the size of the migrant labour force indicates that a level of dependence on it has already developed.

The structural role of migration is particularly evident in the specific sectors in which migrants are involved. In Singapore, migrants outnumber six to four local workers in construction. Taiwan Province of China originally introduced migrant workers because of the need for labour in the construction sector, which currently employs mostly Thai workers. The 1998 Construction Labour Importation Scheme of Hong Kong, China, which was established to overcome labour scarcity in that sector, met strong opposition from unions (*Asian Migration News*, 31 January 1998). Malaysia also depends largely on foreign workers for construction. A large number of construction workers from Myanmar were employed during the infrastructure boom in Thailand in the 1990s. In addition to construction, migrants are employed largely in the manufacturing sector, mostly for small industries as in the case of the Republic of Korea and Taiwan Province of China, but also for major firms as in the case of Nikkeijins (people of Japanese ancestry born and domiciled abroad) employed in the automotive industry in Japan, or Filipinos in the electronics sector in Taiwan Province of China. A third area of employment is the agricultural sector. Operations in plantations in Malaysia or in rice mills and fisheries in Thailand have become dependent on migrant labour.

If migration is a structural component of the receiving Asian economies, both in its occupational dimensions and in its gender consequences, it is also a structural component of the countries of origin, which have become dependent on it. The concept of dependence has both economic and cultural dimensions. The inflow of remittances can be taken as an indicator of the economic relevance of migration. The remittance inflow is significant for all countries of origin (tables 3 and 4). However, for some countries it is decisive, as it constitutes a relevant percentage of the gross national product (GNP). In 1999, remittances were 8.2 per cent of GNP in the Philippines, 6.3 per cent in Sri Lanka, and 3.8 per cent in Bangladesh. Even in a much bigger economy such as India, remittances constituted 2.4 per cent of GNP. Dependence, however, also has a cultural dimension: people and Governments cling to it even when economic benefits decline. The months of the 1997/98 financial crisis in Asia were revealing in that regard. Although countries of destination were quick to act in repatriating migrants and lowering their salary or working standards, the volume of outflows did not decline significantly. On the contrary, Governments in countries of origin were quick either to recommend that migrants remain abroad, even under less favourable conditions (as in the case of the Philippines), or to aim at an increase in the volume of overseas labour (as in the case of Thailand) (Battistella and Asis, 1999).

10

## Table 3. Remittances to selected Asian countries, 1990- 1999

(Million US$)

|      | Bangladesh | India  | Indonesia | Pakistan | Philippines | Sri Lanka | Thailand |
|------|-----------|--------|-----------|----------|-------------|-----------|----------|
| 1990 | 779       | 2 384  | 166       | 1 997    | 1 465       | 401       | 973      |
| 1991 | 769       | 3 289  | 130       | 1 541    | 1 850       | 442       | 1 019    |
| 1992 | 912       | 2 897  | 229       | 1 566    | 2 537       | 548       | 445      |
| 1993 | 1 007     | 3 522  | 346       | 1 446    | 2 587       | 632       | 1 112    |
| 1994 | 1 151     | 5 857  | 449       | 1 749    | 3 452       | 715       | 1 281    |
| 1995 | 1 202     | 6 223  | 651       | 1 712    | 5 360       | 801       | 1 695    |
| 1996 | 1 345     | 8 766  | 796       | 1 284    | 4 875       | 843       | 1 806    |
| 1997 | 1 527     | 10 331 | 725       | 1 707    | 6 799       | 934       | 1 658    |
| 1998 | 1 606     | 9 480  | 959       | NA       | 5 130       | 1 011     | 1 424    |
| 1999 | 1 807     | 11 124 | 1 109     | NA       | 6 896       | 1 068     | 1 460    |

Source: <http://migration.ucdavis.edu>

## Table 4. Percentage GDP growth in selected Asian countries and areas, 1996-2002

| GDP growth | 1996 | 1997 | 1998  | 1999  | 2000 | 2001 | 2002 |
|-----------|------|------|-------|-------|------|------|------|
| Japan[a]  | 5.0  | 1.6  | -2.5  | 0.2   | 1.5  | -0.2 | 0.6  |
| China     | 9.6  | 8.8  | 7.8   | 7.1   | 8.0  | 7.3  | 7.0  |
| Hong Kong, China | 4.5 | 5.0 | -5.3 | 3.0 | 10.5 | -0.4 | 2.0 |
| Republic of Korea | 6.8 | 5.0 | -6.7 | 10.9 | 8.8 | 2.0 | 3.6 |
| Singapore | 7.7  | 8.5  | 0.1   | 5.9   | 9.9  | -3.0 | 1.0  |
| Taiwan Province of China | 6.1 | 6.7 | 4.6 | 5.4 | 5.9 | -2.0 | 2.0 |
| Indonesia | 7.8  | 4.7  | -13.2 | 0.9   | 4.8  | 3.2  | 3.9  |
| Malaysia  | 10.0 | 7.3  | -7.4  | 6.1   | 8.3  | 0.8  | 3.1  |
| Philippines | 5.8 | 5.2 | -0.6  | 3.4   | 4.0  | 2.7  | 3.0  |
| Thailand  | 5.9  | -1.4 | -10.8 | 4.2   | 4.4  | 1.5  | 2.5  |
| Viet Nam  | 9.3  | 8.2  | 4.4   | 4.7   | 6.1  | 6.0  | 6.2  |
| Bangladesh | 4.6 | 5.4  | 5.2   | 4.9   | 5.9  | 6.0  | 5.5  |
| India     | 7.5  | 5.4  | 6.6   | 6.4   | 5.2  | 5.6  | 6.3  |
| Pakistan  | 6.8  | 1.9  | 2.0   | 4.2   | 3.9  | 2.6  | 3.0  |
| Sri Lanka[a] | 3.8 | 6.3 | 4.7  | 4.3   | 6.0  | 3.8  | 4.8  |

Source: Asian Development Outlook 2001 Update, (Manila, Asia Development Bank, 2001).

[a] Tim Holland (2001). "Asia's red-queen economies", Far Eastern Economic Review, 6 September, pp. 54-56.

## Table 5. Annual outflow of migrant workers from selected Asian countries, 1990-1998

(Thousands)

| Year | India | Indonesia | Philippines | Thailand | Pakistan | Bangladesh | Sri Lanka | Total |
|------|-------|-----------|-------------|----------|----------|------------|-----------|---------|
| 1990 | 143.6 | 86.3      | 334.8       | 63.2     | 115.5    | 103.8      | 42.7      | 2 879.7 |
| 1991 | 197.9 | 149.8     | 486.3       | 63.8     | 147.3    | 147.1      | 65.0      | 3 248.2 |
| 1992 | 416.8 | 172.2     | 549.7       | 81.7     | 196.1    | 188.1      | 124.5     | 3 721.1 |
| 1993 | 438.3 | 160.0     | 550.9       | 137.9    | 157.7    | 244.5      | 129.1     | 3 811.1 |
| 1994 | 426.0 | 176.2     | 565.2       | 169.7    | 114.0    | 186.3      | 130.0     | 3 761.4 |
| 1995 | 415.3 | 120.9     | 488.6       | 202.3    | 122.6    | 187.5      | 172.5     | 3 704.7 |
| 1996 | 414.2 | 517.3     | 484.7       | 185.4    | 127.8    | 211.7      | 162.6     | 4 099.7 |
| 1997 | 416.4 | 235.3     | 559.2       | 183.7    | 153.9    | 381.1      | 149.8     | 4 076.4 |
| 1998 | 355.2 | 411.6     | 562.4       | 175.4    | 104.0    | 267.7      | 158.3     | 4 032.6 |

*Source:* Piyasiri Wickramasekara (2000). "Migration workers issues in the ASEAN: Some reflections", in *ILO Asia-Pacific Regional Trade Union Symposium on Migrant Workers,* (Geneva, International Labour Organization).

To summarize this section, it may be said that labour migration, characterized by short contracts and discouragement to integration, involves an annual movement of at least 2 million workers (table 5). However, this is a conservative estimate, relying on the major countries of origin and not including the large movement of unauthorized migrants. Nevertheless, it still constitutes an increase of 44 per cent since 1990. Authorized flows originating from South Asia and Indonesia are directed mostly towards Western Asia and this pattern has not changed significantly for the previous 20 years, except for the increasing number of Bangladeshis in Malaysia; migrants from Thailand go mostly to Asian destinations, while those from the Philippines are almost evenly distributed. The stock of authorized migrants in the major migration-receiving countries of Asia comprises approximately 3.7 million persons (table 1), while the number of unauthorized migrants in the same countries is 2.4 million (table 2). However, the estimate of unauthorized migrants in South Asia is not included.

### Highly skilled migrants

The 1990s ushered in a "new economy" with its spectacular increase in investments in products and services related to information technology (IT). With the rise of the new economy, opportunities for employment also shifted, as a shortage of highly skilled IT workers was felt in all developed economies. Developing countries saw a "window of opportunity" and shifted emphasis in their educational systems towards computer-related studies. India, in particular,

12

but also the Philippines began churning out IT graduates every year who intended to work mostly abroad. Less than 30 per cent landed a job at home (Robles and Kapoor, 2001). A true education for export was established, and soon it was threatened by the burst of the IT bubble.

The circulation of highly skilled workers in the region is not a recent phenomenon. Loosely defined as people with a university degree or with extensive experience in a particular field (OECD, 1998, p. 188), highly skilled workers have increasingly been in demand thanks to the expansion of transnational corporations. The movement of highly skilled workers has been examined particularly in relation to specific flows: that of corporations from East Asia to other regions; the movement of capital from Taiwan Province of China and Hong Kong, China towards mainland China; the mobility of the workforce within South-East Asia; and the reverse flow involving the children of Asian migrants returning from North America (Iredale, 2000). China has adopted incentives to facilitate return among its estimated 250,000 students abroad (*Asian Migration News,* 31 August 2001). Very significant for their economic and cultural impact, highly skilled workers are much fewer in number compared with migrant workers, and far less problematic.

The major competition for IT workers comes from countries in North America and Europe. Perhaps 10 per cent of the 350,000 IT workers in Silicon Valley are Chinese and Indian nationals (*Migration News,* November·2001). The most outspoken country in Asia favouring the immigration of IT workers is Singapore, the Prime Minister of which openly bids to lure technicians from India. In fact, the number of highly skilled – judged by the number of employment pass holders – increased in Singapore from 20,000 in the 1980s to 110,000 in 2000. At the same time, the influx of foreign talent is generating resentment as competition for jobs increases, possibly leading some local citizens to migrate to other countries (Hui, 2001). To help to save local jobs while attracting foreign talent, Singapore raised the minimum salary for an employment pass from S$ 2,000 to S$ 2,500 (US$1 = S$1.70), effective 1 December 2001 (*Asian Migration News,* 15 October 2001).

If highly skilled workers are possibly in the proportion of one to six in Singapore, they are far less significant in Malaysia, which has a much larger migrant population. Nevertheless, professional (or expatriate) migrants had increased to 61,300 in 1990; however, their numbers decreased again to 16,173 in 1999 (Kanapathy, 2001).

The circulation of highly skilled workers will suffer more than the migration of the low skilled owing to the vagaries of economic tendencies. However, it must be considered an established trend, dependent also on policy directions. The Asia-Pacific Economic Cooperation (APEC) forum tried to facilitate the flow of professionals by establishing a human resource development programme and providing an APEC card for easy travelling. However, differences in training and qualifications dampen the capacity of Governments to intervene in an effort to respond to skill shortages in the region (Iredale, 2000).

## Refugees and emigrants

At the start of January 2001, the Office of the United Nations High Commissioner for Refugees (UNHCR) estimated that Asia had the largest number of persons of concern to UNHCR (8.4 million, which is equal to 44.5 per cent of the total).[2] The largest group of refugees is from Afghanistan (3.6 million); they are living in the Islamic Republic of Iran and Pakistan. In addition to those who had not returned after the end of the war with the former Union of Soviet Socialist Republics (USSR) (1.6 million), they include those who left later and those displaced by drought. The recent war against the Taliban regime has increased the number of Afghanis seeking refuge in neighbouring Pakistan, particularly Afghanis from the country's southern provinces. Repatriation of a number of the 2.3 million refugees in the Islamic Republic of Iran was begun in the Spring of 2002. A second large group comprises Iraqis hosted mostly in the Islamic Republic of Iran (512,800). Smaller but significant groups of refugees include people from Bhutan in Nepal (perhaps 100,000), Rohingyas (Muslims) from Myanmar in Bangladesh (22,000), and Karens from Myanmar in Thailand.

Mention should also be made of the flow of migrants from Asia who resettle every year in North American countries, Australia and New Zealand. This flow involved 322,048 persons in 1998[3] (27,119 in Australia, 17,927 in New Zealand, 190,807 in the United States of America and 84,197 – including also Pacific islanders – in Canada). This means that 32 per cent of the settlers came from Asian countries. Among the top countries of origin were China (66,106), India (56,249), the Philippines (46,664) and Viet Nam (19,882). This flow is set to continue for some time, since family reunification occupies a significant place in the migration policies of immigration countries.

---

[2] <http:// www.unhcr.org>

[3] Figures have been taken from the websites of each country's Immigration Department.

## Unauthorized migration and trafficking

Unauthorized migration is a companion phenomenon in all migration flows. There is no country which is immune from unauthorized migration, whether in the form of unauthorized entry, unauthorized stay or unauthorized employment. In Asia, this form of migration often took place before formal migration policies were established, and it continued in the presence of migration policies that do not adequately reflect the interplay between the demand for migrant labour and migration pressure.

Unauthorized migration follows some distinct regional patterns. In East Asia, where countries of destination do not necessarily border with the countries of origin, it occurs mostly in the form of overstaying the terms granted in one's visa or by taking unauthorized employment. In South-East Asia, where the main countries of destination share a border with the country of origin (such as Thailand and Myanmar or Malaysia and Indonesia), many unauthorized migrants enter and stay without proper documentation. Unauthorized migration in South Asia, mostly from Bangladesh and Nepal to India, also follows this pattern, a situation complicated by the remnants of historical issues.

By definition, unauthorized migration escapes proper monitoring. Therefore, estimates on unauthorized migrants vary considerably according to the purpose of the estimate. However, reliability is higher when figures refer to overstayers, as in the case of Japan and the Republic of Korea.

In Japan, 51,459 unauthorized migrants were deported in 2000, down from 55,167 in 1999. Among them, 40,756 had overstayed their visas and 9,186 had entered the country illegally (*Asian Migration News*, 31 May 2001). Unauthorized migrants totalled 251,697 in January 2000, and continued to decrease. A small number may qualify for special residence, granted to 6,930 in 2001 (*Asian Migration News*, 15 July 2001). In the Republic of Korea, after a reduction in this type of migration caused by the 1997/98 financial crisis, unauthorized migrants increased again to 220,000 in August 2001 (*Asian Migration News*, 31 August 2001). The number of unauthorized migrants in Malaysia varies widely, from 600,000 to 1 million. However, there is agreement that unauthorized migrants are mostly from Indonesia, and that one fifth of them are in Sabah (*Asian Migration News*, 31 August 2001). Thailand will initiate a regularization process of perhaps 1 million workers, more than 80 per cent of whom are from Myanmar, living in Thailand without authorization. The registration, effective for six months and renewable, would cost 3,250 baht per worker (or 4,450 baht for a year-long stay)

(US$1 = around 42 baht) and will be coordinated by the Ministry of Labour (*Asian Migration News,* 15 September 2001). Unauthorized migration can also be considered from the perspective of the country of origin, when migrants go abroad without passing through paper systems. For example, the Philippines acknowledges that perhaps 1.9 million Filipinos abroad are not in a regular status (Battistella, 2001).

A specific movement of mostly unauthorized migration has developed within the Commonwealth of Independent States (CIS). After the collapse of the USSR, there was a significant relocation of ethnic Russians and others (4.7 million according to estimates of the International Organization for Migration (IOM)) who found it difficult to remain within the newly independent countries that were redeveloping a national identity. Some 73 centres were established to temporarily host Russians before relocation (IOM, 2000a). The Russian Federation also issued permits to hire migrant labour (100,000 in 1997). However, the most significant movement involved unauthorized migrants (between 700,000 and 1.5 million), including overstaying students and workers, as well as people coming from neighbouring provinces of China (IOM, 2000a). Taking advantage of the porous borders, CIS countries are also used as transit countries for migrants attempting to enter Eastern Europe. Coming mostly from South Asia, they end up in the Russian Federation and the Ukraine on their way to the Czech Republic, Hungary and Poland. CIS countries found themselves ill equipped to respond to this unprecedented human movement. Unauthorized migration is leading to the establishment of foreign communities and the creation of ethnic tensions. Some States, such as Kazakhstan and Azerbaijan, have concluded visa agreements with Asian countries, negatively affecting efforts to combat unauthorized migration (Lebedev, 1999). In 1998, nine CIS countries – Georgia, Turkmenistan and Uzbekistan did not participate – concluded an agreement to combat unauthorized migration, while pressure from the European Union and Baltic countries was applied to re-admit unauthorized migrants from third countries to be repatriated to their countries of origin (Lebedev, 1999).

Unauthorized migration is further complicated by two subtypes of movement: the smuggling of migrants and the trafficking of persons, especially women and children. The recent adoption of two protocols to the United Nations Convention against Transnational Organized Crime has helped to clarify the definitions of the various aspects, which have in common the crossing of international borders. The smuggling of migrants involves securing their illegal entry to a country for the purpose of obtaining financial or material benefit. Trafficking in persons covers various aspects of this transnational movement, particularly of women and children, in which some use of force, coercion, abduction, fraud or deception is involved for the purpose of exploitation (for prostitution, forced labour, slavery or other such purposes). The consent of the victim is immaterial. In both cases, migrants are not criminally liable; rather, they are victims in need of protection.

Trafficking has attracted considerable attention in the region, with programmes implemented by international organizations such as the International Labour Organization and IOM, but also by networks of non-governmental organizations (NGOs). They have focused on children trafficked for prostitution; the Mekong region is a particularly sensitive area, with large numbers trafficked for prostitution in Cambodia and Thailand.[4] Other forms of exploitation have been uncovered, such as the case of children trafficked for bonded labour, or under the disguise of adoption (IOM, 2000b).

Trafficking of women develops in the region at the fringe of the various movements which take women into difficult labour conditions and shady occupations, such as entertainment, or into marital arrangements which channel women into prostitution. The traditional nodes of this trafficking are India and Japan as destination countries and Bangladesh, Nepal and the Philippines as countries of origin. Two flows have also developed from CIS countries towards Western Europe and East Asia. According to a project implemented by Johns Hopkins University, perhaps 200,000 Nepalese girls are sexual slaves in India. However, Thailand serves as a country of origin, destination and transit of a complex web of trafficking, involving also the neighbouring countries of Indochina. Trafficking also occurs in other countries. Recently, *The Jakarta Post* called attention to the phenomenon in Indonesia, where women are trafficked for 350,000 rupiahs (US$1 = Rp 8,700), less than the cost of a goat (Saraswati, 2001).

"Trafficking in human beings is the fastest growing form of organized crime", stated the Under-Secretary-General of the United Nations Office for Drug Control and Drug Prevention.[5] This is particularly clear in the growth of criminal activities for the smuggling of migrants. Flows between Indonesia and Malaysia, between Myanmar and Thailand, but also between China and Japan are possible because of organizations that possess the information and contacts to ensure the arrival of migrants at the country of destination. Perhaps the most lucrative route for

---

[4] *<http://www.sais-jhu.edu/protectionproject/index.html>* and *<http://www.protectionproject.org/main1.htm>*

[5] From address by Pino Arlacchi to the Permanent Council of the Organization for Security and Cooperation in Europe, 1 November 2001, Vienna.

trafficking is the one of Chinese migrants – perhaps 50,000 a year, mostly from the province of Fujian – towards North America and Europe (Skeldon, 2000). The tragedy of the 56 persons who died inside a lorry in Dover, United Kingdom has remained as one of the most gruesome episodes of a phenomenon which goes largely undetected. The recent sinking of a boat off Indonesia, in which 370 migrants heading for Christmas Island (Australia) perished, has uncovered a smuggling route which originates in Afghanistan, Iraq and the Islamic Republic of Iran towards Australia via Malaysia and Indonesia. The position of Malaysia on curbing this flow, which could potentially increase with the hostilities and dislocations in Afghanistan, has caused diplomatic friction with Australia (Elegant, 2001); a hard line against boat people and asylum applicants became a crucial issue in a recent electoral campaign.

To help formulate effective policies against unauthorized migration, it is important to know the perspective of the migrants involved. That perspective was sought in a recent research project on unauthorized migration in South-East Asia. One of the intentions was to explore the reasons why migrants take the illegal route towards migration. The hypothesis was that it could be because of a lack of information on the proper procedures, because of deceit by agents and officials, or simply because of convenience. Results from 101 migrants interviewed in the Philippines indicated that those migrants in general did not lack information, which at the initial stage was provided by social networks, and then was supplemented by recruiting agencies. Unauthorized migration (in its various forms) was chosen to get around the restrictions of the migration process and gain admission to countries such as Italy, Japan and the Republic of Korea. When the irregularity committed consisted of entering with a visitor's visa and overstaying, migrants could rely on social networks to facilitate their insertion in the country. Illegal recruiters were chosen in 50 per cent of the cases and 80 per cent of the migrants who utilized their services felt that they had been victimized by them (Battistella and Asis, 2001).

Unauthorized migration has been met in recent years by emphasis on stricter border control (India completed the fencing of its remaining 797 km of border with Bangladesh); increasing penalties against employers who hire unauthorized migrants; tough measures against agents who help migrants enter the country illegally; and punishment of unauthorized migrants. In Singapore, tenants who provided housing to migrants without checking the legality of their documents were also arrested. The small and short-lived success against unauthorized migration (in Thailand it is often said that deported migrants return after a few days) reveals that unauthorized migration is also a structural component of labour mobility. To put it in different terms, it is the response of migrants to structural deficiencies in the migration process in the region. The following observations are worth considering (IOM, 1999).

(a) Although unauthorized migration exists in all countries of the region, the great majority of such movement occurs in only three countries: India, Malaysia and Thailand. Why does such an imbalance occur?

(b) Unauthorized migration in the form of overstaying is a response to restrictive migration policies limiting the duration of overseas labour in the country of destination. Can such a system be maintained without producing unauthorized migration?

(c) Unauthorized migration is possible thanks to the mediation of recruiters, travel agents, immigration officials and job placement agencies. Can unauthorized migration be reduced without adversely affecting the migration "industry"?

(d) Unauthorized migration rests on the availability of work opportunities. Is it possible to curb unauthorized migration without addressing irregularities in the labour market?

(e) Unauthorized migration involves at least a country of origin and a country of destination (and sometimes a transit country). However, policies to combat unauthorized migration are normally taken unilaterally by individual countries. How effective can such policies be?

## HOW WILL MIGRATION TRENDS DEVELOP?

In describing the major trends of migration in Asia, their structural nature has been emphasized, which leads both the countries of origin and the countries of destination to some degree of dependence on migration. In that regard, migration in its major forms seems already to have become a permanent feature of Asian societies, albeit composed of people in precarious living and working conditions. Nevertheless, the volume and direction of migration flows as well as their composition are subject to changes in relation to economic and political factors. For instance, the dispute between the Philippines and Taiwan Province of China over an airline agreement led to a temporary halt in the hiring of Filipino workers in manufacturing occupations and opened an opportunity for migrants from Viet

Nam to take their place. Three major factors which will influence migration in Asia in the future are considered below.

## Demographic trends

Although demographic factors do not generate migration, and demographic disparities are insufficient in the determination of migration flows, demographic trends are important because of their impact on migration propensity (Massey and others, 1998). Hugo (1998) observed that the rate of growth of the labour force in the least developed economies is higher than that of the total population, whereas in most developed countries, the opposite occurs, and this trend will exacerbate in the next two decades. A renowned report on replacement migration (United Nations, 2000) painted a drastic picture of the number of migrants needed between now and the year 2050 just to maintain a constant total population. Japan would need 343,000 migrants every year, while the Republic of Korea would need 30,000. A study by Asian Demographics Ltd. estimates that Singapore will need to boost its workforce by about 90,000 a year to maintain growth rates (*Asian Migration News,* 15 September 2001). It is unlikely that migration flows of such dimensions will take place, but it is possible that Governments, particularly in Japan and the Republic of Korea will give in to some demands from the business sector for foreign labour (*Asian Migration News,* 15 October 2001).

## Economic recession

The world economy experienced a sharp decline in output at the beginning of 2001. The International Monetary Fund revised its global growth projection for 2002 from 4.2 to 3.2 per cent. More specifically, it has downgraded by two percentage points the growth projection for the United States economy. At the same time, the Japanese economy is not emerging from its long crisis and Europe does not seem capable of offsetting the decline occurring elsewhere (IMF, 2001). The impact of the slowdown has already been experienced by the Asian economies, where only China continues to maintain high growth, together with several South Asian economies, which are marginally dependent on technology (table 4). It all started with the crash of the electronic Nasdaq Stock Market, a symbol of the spectacular growth of the United States economy in the 1990s. The burst of the new economic bubble had an immediate impact on Asian economies, largely dependent on the export of electronic and IT products. Singapore and Taiwan Province of China are already experiencing recession and Malaysia and the Philippines, both with 60 per cent of their exports comprising semiconductors, microchips and other electronics, must cope with sluggish demand. The Republic of Korea is in a slightly better position, but also remains overdependent on the export of semiconductors (Holland, 2001). The threat of global terrorism further diminished confidence, delaying the recovery.

As the decline is severe in the electronic and IT sectors, it is expected that some demand for migrants in the manufacturing sector will decrease. From January to August 2001, 8,000 Malaysians in Singapore were retrenched (*Asian Migration News,* 15 October 2001). Migrants are not widely employed in high-tech industries, except perhaps in Taiwan Province of China. In fact, the reduction of migrants in manufacturing in Taiwan Province of China was already being experienced for some months, owing to the transfer of factories to mainland China.[6] However, the flow of highly skilled workers in the region might also experience some decline, as unemployed workers demand the jobs held by foreigners. This is already happening in Singapore, although the Government maintains its policy to attract foreign talents (Dawes, 2001). A different impact is observed in Hong Kong, China, where specialized workers are losing their jobs as a result of companies relocating to the mainland, although they might regain them if they are willing to migrate to the mainland (Finer, 2001).

A general decline of the economy could certainly affect the construction sector, as investments decline and consumers tend to hold on to savings and to defer home improvements. This should lead to a decrease in the number of migrants with construction jobs in Singapore, perhaps less so in Malaysia, where most construction workers come from Indonesia, not necessarily with authorization, and can fall back into the informal economy.

The service sector could experience a backlash as households conclude that they can no longer afford a foreign domestic worker. Worries are expressed particularly in places with high concentrations of domestic workers such as Hong Kong, China; and Singapore (Sheehan, 2001). On the one hand, large-scale retrenchment of domestic workers is improbable, as it did not happen even during the 1997/98 financial crisis. What happened, instead, was a moratorium on the levy granted in Singapore and a decline of 5 per cent in the salaries of domestic workers in Hong Kong, China. Migrants will try to accept lower wages[7] in order to maintain employment. On the other hand, the encouragement of the

---

[6] Migrants in manufacturing jobs declined from 58.9 per cent of the total in May 2000 to 54.3 in May 2001 (CIA, 2001).

[7] Monthly salaries for Filipina domestic workers might be as low as HK$ 2,000 (US$ 1 = HK$ 7.78) on the black market (*Asian Migration News,* 31 July 2001).

21

Government, providing training to local women,[8] might produce a change from full-time foreign workers to part-time local domestic workers (*Asian Migration News*, 15 October 2001).

The lowering of wages and living conditions is already being planned in Taiwan Province of China, where board and lodging (between NT$ 4,000 and NT$ 6,000) would be deducted from minimum wages (NT$ 15,840), saving business NT$ 10 billion (US$ 1 = NT$ 34.6). Lower income should be compensated by lower brokerage fees, which are difficult to control. As unemployment rises in all the societies concerned, a wave of repatriations is to be expected, starting with unauthorized migrants. Nevertheless, migration pressure will not decline, as employment opportunities will not improve in the major places of origin, such as Indonesia, the Philippines and Taiwan Province of China.

Some lessons learned from the impact of the 1997/98 financial crisis on migration might help in understanding the short-term development of current trends. One such lesson is that *migrants do not compete with nationals in the labour market*. As previous studies have indicated, in the unskilled labour market migrants do not substitute – they complement – the local labour force.[9] In Thailand, all attempts to give migrants' jobs to local workers failed, regardless of the incentives that were offered. Such competition is perceived differently in the highly skilled sector. However, highly skilled migrants are also not in competition with nationals because of the scarcity of their talents, as explicitly shown in the case of Singapore (Dawes, 2001). A second lesson indicates that *migrants tend to remain in the country of destination even when conditions worsen*. This conclusion is not derived from accurate data, but from the large number of migrants caught in an irregular situation or from the "revolving-door" experience of those who were repatriated and soon afterward returned. On the basis of those two lessons, it is possible that the hopefully temporary recession will cause only a temporary disruption of migratory flows, affecting some sectors more than others, but not altering the major trends.

---

[8] The Government initially considered financing the training of local domestic workers through a levy of HK$ 400 imposed on employers of foreign domestic workers *(Asian Migration News*, 15 August 2001).

[9] However, a recent study in Taiwan Province of China revealed that migrants have an impact on the rising unemployment rate among low-skilled nationals in migrant-dependent industries (construction, manufacturing and domestic services) (Tsay and Pin, 2001). Borjas (1999, p. 10) also contends that migrants harm the economic opportunities of the least skilled.

## Political factors

Recently, the migration policies of some countries in the region have acquired an increasingly restrictive character. Japan has revised its policy on overstayers; they can be imprisoned even if caught after three years of permanence in that country. The Republic of Korea has not proceeded with the introduction of a work permit system, because of the opposition of small businesses. Taiwan Province of China lowered wages for its migrants. On the positive side, Singapore has increased penalties against employers who abuse domestic workers, while Thailand is regularizing its large number of unauthorized migrants, adopting a work permit system and providing migrants with a minimum wage, housing and medical care (*Asian Migration News*, 15 July 2001).

Migration policies remain solidly a national affair. International initiatives, such as a proposed United Nations conference on migration, have been shelved. Even regional initiatives, such as the Bangkok Declaration and the Asian Regional Initiative against Trafficking in Women and Children, have not prospered. It is difficult to see any country with sufficient resolve to provide leadership in this sector. Although globalization has had major impacts on the movement of capital and equipment, Governments have not opened their countries' doors to the international movement of workers.

Stability in the region, which had become more solid with changes of leadership in Indonesia, Japan and the Philippines, is now threatened by the imponderable consequences of the war in Afghanistan. However, massive dislocation of migrants as the one produced by the Persian Gulf war in 1991 will probably not occur.

# MIGRATION AND POVERTY

Intuitively, there is a tight linkage between migration and poverty. Migration can be considered an attempt to escape poverty. When asked about the determinants of migration, many will simply answer "poverty". However, this generally held impression needs further examination. Do the data support the thesis that migration is caused by poverty? Conversely, is migration decreasing poverty in the countries of origin? Finally, how is the discussion contributing to the issue of poverty reduction?

**Table 6. Poverty and other social indicators in selected Asian countries and areas (latest year)**

| Country/ area | Less than US$1 a day | | Country poverty line | | HDI rank[a] | HPI rank[a] | GDP per capita[a] | Merchandise Export |
|---|---|---|---|---|---|---|---|---|
| | Incidence (%) | No. of poor (millions) | Incidence (%) | No. of poor (millions) | | | (PPP US$) 1999 | as percentage of GDP[b] |
| Japan | | | | | 9 | | 24 898 | |
| Republic of Korea | | | 7.4 | 3.5 | 27 | | 15 712 | 38.4 |
| Singapore | | | | | 26 | | 20 767 | 149.5 |
| Hong Kong, China | | | | | 24 | | 22 090 | 124.6 |
| Taiwan Province of China | | | 0.6 | 0.1 | | | | 63.9 |
| China | 18.5 | 233.6 | | 55.4 | 87 | 24 | 3 617 | 23.1 |
| Bangladesh | 29.1 | 37.9 | 44.7 | 58.2 | 132 | 73 | 1 483 | |
| India | 44.2 | 442.9 | 26.1 | 261.6 | 115 | 55 | 2 248 | |
| Nepal | 37.7 | 8.6 | 42.0 | 9.6 | 129 | 77 | 1 237 | |
| Pakistan | 31.0 | 42.6 | 32.2 | 44.3 | 127 | 65 | 1 834 | |
| Sri Lanka | 6.6 | 1.3 | 26.7 | 5.2 | 81 | 31 | 3 279 | 33.5 |
| Cambodia | | | 35.9 | 4.4 | 121 | 78 | 1 361 | 44.5 |
| Lao People's Democratic Republic | 26.3 | 1.4 | 38.6 | 2.0 | 131 | 66 | 1 471 | |
| Myanmar | | | | | 118 | 43 | 1 027 | |
| Viet Nam | | | 37.0 | 28.7 | 101 | 45 | 1 860 | |
| Indonesia | 7.7 | 16.2 | 23.4 | 49.3 | 102 | 38 | 2 857 | 40.5 |
| Malaysia | | | 8.1 | 1.9 | 56 | 13 | 8 209 | 109.9 |
| Philippines | | | 36.8 | 28.9 | 70 | 23 | 3 805 | 53.7 |
| Thailand | 2 | 1.2 | 12.9 | 8.1 | 66 | 21 | 6 132 | 56.7 |

*Source: Key Indicators of Developing Asian and Pacific Countries 2001, Volume 32,* (Manila, Asian Development Bank, 2001).

[a] *Human Development Report 2001,* (New York, UNDP, 2001).
[b] *Asian Development Outlook 20001 Update,* (Manila, Asian Development Bank, 2001).

## The impact of poverty on migration

The presentation of migration trends has illustrated that migration originates from countries in South and South-East Asia and is directed towards the countries of East and South-East Asia. Table 6 shows the differentials in terms of GDP per capita and poverty incidence between origins and destinations. However, as specified in the theoretical note, the existence of differentials does not in itself generate human mobility. If it were so, the distribution of migrants by nationality should reflect the distribution of the poor in the Asian and Pacific region. In fact, the reality is different. Some countries with a high incidence of poverty (Bangladesh for instance) do not have the highest flow of migrants in the region, while others (Cambodia, the Lao People's Democratic Republic, Viet Nam) play only a marginal role in the supply of migrants. In addition, the country with the most established and consistent system of labour migration and with the highest diversification of destinations – the Philippines – has a level of poverty lower than that of Bangladesh, India and Pakistan. Thus, while poverty creates the premise for the decision to migrate, it does not in itself lead one to the decision to migrate.

Remaining at the macro level, it is important to observe that practically all countries in the region are involved in the migration process, although at different rates, and their involvement will develop according to a transition pattern dependent on this income level. According to Rowlands (1998, p. 15), emigration is highest for countries with per capita income levels of around $3,100 (1990 adjusted), with the range of estimated peaks from $2,260 to $3,865. Data on GDP per capita in table 6 confirm Rowlands' conclusion, with the exception of China, because of migration policies. The same data would suggest that perhaps the Philippines has reached its migration peak while flows from other countries will possibly increase, policies permitting.

Among the reasons for the lack of a deterministic link between poverty and migration, in addition to the role of migration policies, is the fact that migration requires financial and human capital, which the poor do not possess. Most migration in the region takes place with the involvement of various intermediaries (labour recruiters, brokers, travel agents, government officials). The involvement of the private sector in a field of competition among agents and among countries and areas has made migration an expensive enterprise. Fees vary according to the places of origin and destination as well as the wages that the migrants will earn. For instance, in the case of the Philippines, placement agencies usually are allowed to charge a fixed amount, i.e. 5,000 pesos (US$ 1 = 57.7 pesos) plus one month's salary for most destinations, although some destinations charge additional

## Table 7. Migration and poverty in the Philippines

| Region | Distribution of Overseas Filipino Workers (%) 1999 | Males 1999 | Females 1999 | Poverty incidence[a] 1997 | Distribution of remittances (%) 1999 | Males 1999 | Females 1999 | Average remittance (Pesos) 1999 |
|---|---|---|---|---|---|---|---|---|
| National Capital Region | 19.1 | 23.8 | 13.9 | 6.4 | 25.7 | 29.6 | 17.0 | 57 191 |
| Cordillera | 2.6 | 1.5 | 4.0 | 42.5 | 2.1 | 1.2 | 4.2 | 32 675 |
| Ilocos Region | 9.6 | 5.1 | 14.5 | 37.8 | 6.1 | 3.9 | 10.8 | 26 656 |
| Cagayan Valley | 4.2 | 1.5 | 7.2 | 32.1 | 2.3 | 0.4 | 6.5 | 23 271 |
| Central Luzon | 14.5 | 16.5 | 12.3 | 15.4 | 13.8 | 14.4 | 12.5 | 38 147 |
| Southern Tagalog | 17.2 | 20.8 | 13.3 | 25.7 | 19.9 | 21.2 | 16.9 | 48 707 |
| Bicol Region | 3.8 | 4.2 | 3.4 | 50.1 | 3.4 | 3.4 | 3.4 | 35 406 |
| Western Visayas | 9.0 | 9.1 | 8.9 | 39.9 | 10.4 | 10.5 | 10.2 | 48 124 |
| Central Visayas | 5.4 | 6.8 | 3.8 | 34.4 | 5.3 | 6.4 | 2.8 | 45 252 |
| Eastern Visayas | 2.1 | 2.6 | 1.6 | 40.8 | 2.0 | 2.5 | 0.9 | 43 114 |
| Western Mindanao | 3.4 | 2.0 | 4.8 | 40.1 | 1.4 | 1.1 | 2.2 | 31 853 |
| Northern Mindanao | 1.2 | 0.9 | 1.8 | 47.0 | 1.4 | 0.8 | 2.7 | 53 431 |
| Southern Mindanao | 3.0 | 1.5 | 4.4 | 38.2 | 2.6 | 1.7 | 4.5 | 38 347 |
| Central Mindanao | 1.8 | 1.5 | 2.4 | 50.0 | 1.5 | 0.9 | 2.7 | 37 589 |
| Autonomous Region for Muslim Mindanao | 1.5 | 0.5 | 2.6 | 57.3 | 0.6 | 0.2 | 1.5 | 17 258 |
| Caraga | 1.5 | 2.0 | 1.0 | | 1.6 | 1.9 | 1.1 | 38 727 |
| Total | 100 | 100 | 100 | 31.8 | 100 | 100 | 100 | 42 760 |

*Source:* Calculated from *1999 Survey on Overseas Filipinos*, (Manila, National Statisticial Office, 2001).

[a] *2000 Philippine Statistical Yearbook*, (Manila, National Statisticial Coordination Board, 2000).

fees. In general, Governments that allow fees to be charged to migrant workers also have a hard time in keeping the fees within the established limits. In the case of unauthorized migration, the cost of obtaining a job abroad is generally higher, as revealed by many migrants caught in the smuggling process. There is no definitive analysis of the actual impact of fees in the selection process of migrants. However, to avoid cutting off the poor who could not avail themselves of overseas work opportunities, recruiting agencies have arranged a system of salary deduction, whereby fees are not paid before going abroad, but over a period of time while the migrant is working on site. If this system has expanded the opportunities of the poor for migration, it also places them in a situation of indenture, as they have to accept all conditions because of the debt they incur to the recruiter.

In spite of the various schemes facilitating access to migration, some data from the Philippines indicate that migrants are not coming from the poorest regions. Table 7 shows that the majority of migrants are coming from Metro Manila and its surrounding regions, which are also the regions with the lowest incidence of poverty. It should be remembered, however, that the same regions were the destinations of internal migration in previous decades. Thus, one could infer that migrants are indeed coming from the poorest regions, but in a two-stage process: first comes internal migration and then international migration. Saith (1997) concluded that it is not possible to speak of internal migration as a stepping-stone towards international migration. Nevertheless, research projects have indicated that at least one third of migrants are first involved in internal migration (Asis, 2001).

## The impact of migration on poverty

At the macro level, it is expected that migration, through remittances and the compound effect they have, will contribute to poverty reduction in the countries of origin. In general terms, remittances have certainly contributed significantly to the economies of the countries of origin. Without remittances, the economy of those countries would have been much more problematic. It is also obvious that without remittances many families would have sustained harsher living conditions. However, macro data do not present the actual situation for those who are below the poverty line.

The following provides some analysis utilizing data from the Philippines. Table 7 indicates that the regions of origin of migrants were also the regions that captured the largest portion of remittances. More than half the remittances are destined for Metro Manila and the surrounding areas. In a more detailed analysis, Saith (1997, p. 27) concluded that remittances "accrue disproportionately to the richer regions, sectors and classes". The opposite, instead, is true with regard to domestic transfers, which are directed mostly to the poorest regions and the poorest classes. It could be argued that the idea of a "trickle-down" effect of remittances could possibly be supported by taking a reverse stepping stone: with the remittances being accrued first to the regions of origin of migrants, and then to the regions of their birth, where other family members are still living. However, adequate data to sustain this hypothesis are not available.

What is available, instead, is the different pattern of remittances according to sex. Although the estimate of female overseas workers is just slightly lower than that of males (48 and 52 per cent, respectively), males obtained 69 per cent of the remittances. This is the result of the disproportionate employment of female migrants in low-wage occupations, such as domestic work. However, table 7 indicates that women are significantly less present in the richer regions. Consequently, the impact of female migration on poverty in terms of direct impact on the poorer regions is more significant than that of males. Once again, the significance of women for poverty reduction, supported by studies in other fields, is confirmed also with regard to migration.

## Absolute or relative poverty?

The first section has discussed the linkage between absolute poverty, whether determined according to international or national poverty lines, and migration. However, an equally important concept is that of self-rated poverty. It is of less use for international comparison, but is highly revealing in capturing the sentiment of those who are directly involved. In the Philippines, for instance, various surveys using this concept have concluded that between 60 and 70 per cent of persons considered themselves to be poor. A survey on the well-being of Filipinos reported that 45 per cent of families considered themselves as poor (SyCip and others, 2000). This is particularly relevant as it reflects the concept of relative deprivation, already mentioned in the theoretical note and which functions as an important mechanism for migration propensity. In other words, migration occurs because of the perception of relative poverty that people experience. If absolute poverty is not a mechanism sufficient to generate migration, relative poverty is, and one could argue that migration propensity occurs in that proportion of people who consider themselves poor but who do not fall below the poverty line. Likewise, migration, with its uneven distribution of benefits, contributes to the relative poverty perception, thus providing a mechanism for the continuation of the migration process. Again, empirical research would be necessary to test this hypothesis.

## CONCLUSIONS AND RECOMMENDATIONS

Migration is an established social phenomenon in Asia, involving a considerable number of persons from developing countries employed in a variety of occupations. Both for countries of origin and countries of destination, migration has acquired a structural role, although of different proportion and significance. Consequently, migration deserves to be discussed at the regional level to ensure its orderly development and the protection of migrants. Countries should consider ratifying the International Convention on the Protection of the Rights of All Migrant Workers and Members of Their Families (adopted by United Nations General Assembly resolution 45/158 of 18 December 1990), which provides a framework for orderly migration.

In the region, unauthorized migration is the result of a multiplicity of factors, including inadequately restrictive policies and the role of intermediaries. Smuggling migrants across borders and the trafficking of persons, particularly women and children, constitute the worst forms of unauthorized migration. Cooperation should be established to eliminate the causes of unauthorized migration, particularly through the establishment and implementation of congruent migration policies. Countries should consider ratifying the International Convention against Transnational Organized Crime and its Protocols and combat organized crime networks involved in smuggling and the trafficking of migrants, while ensuring that the rights of the victims are protected.

Migration is an expression of the resolve of people to escape poverty. Recognizing the role that migration plays in the economies of developing countries, regional policies designed to decrease poverty in the region should reflect also the role of migration. However, as migration has only a partial impact on the direct reduction of poverty and a greater impact in the indirect reduction of poverty, adequate development policies, which would best utilize migrants' remittances and skills, are even more important than specific migration policies.

Taking advantage of the greater mobility of capital over labour, adequate programmes in human capital development and utilization in countries of origin should be put in place to provide alternatives to labour mobility, particularly of highly skilled IT workers.

Considering the relevance of women in migration and the crucial role that women play in reducing household poverty, migration policies should be gender sensitive and ensure the protection of women.

Specific attention should be given to ensure that migrants who settle in the country of destination (such as foreign spouses) enjoy equality of treatment with nationals and are not rendered poor because of migration.

## REFERENCES

*Asian Migration News* (various issues, 2001). <*http://www.scalabrini.org/~smc/ amnews /amnews.htm>*.

Asis, Maruja M.B. (2001a). "Irregular migration from the perspective of a country of origin: The Philippines", Quezon City, Philippines, Scalabrini Migration Center, (unpublished).

Asis, Maruja M.B. (2001b). "The return migration of Filipino women migrants: Home, but not for good," in, Christina Willie and Basia Passl (eds.), *Female Labour Migration in South-East Asia: Change and Continuity,* (Bangkok, Asian Research Centre for Migration).

Battistella, Graziano (2001). "Migration 2000 in Asia: A year in review", *Asian Migrant*, vol. 14, No. 1.

Battistella, Graziano and Maruja M.B. Asis (1999). *The Crisis and Migration in Asia.* (Quezon City, Philippines, Scalabrini Migration Center).

Battistella, Graziano and Maruja M.B. Asis (eds.) (2003). "Irregular migration: The underside of the global migration of Filipinos", in *Unauthorized Migration in Southeast Asia,* (Quezon City, the Philippines, Scalabrini Migration Center).

Borjas, George J. (1999). *Heaven's Door: Immigration Policy and the American Economy,* (Princeton, New Jersey, Princeton University Press).

Central Intelligence Agency (CIA). The World Factbook 2000, <*http:// www.odci.gov/cia/ publications/factbook/index.html >*.

Choi, Jin Ho (2001). "International migration, human resource development and migration policy in Korea", *Asian and Pacific Migration Journal,* vol. 10, Nos. 3-4, pp. 463-484.

Dawes, Joseph (2001). "Beware the alien invasion", *Asiaweek*, 14 September.

Elegant, Simon (2001). "Shipwrecked", *Time*, 5 November.

Ernsberger Jr., Richard (2001). "The Spread of China Inc.", *Newsweek*, 3 September.

Finer, Jonathan (2001). "Migration season for jobs", *Far Eastern Economic Review*, 1 November.

Holland, Tim (2001). "Asia's red-queen economies", *Far Eastern Economic Review*, 6 September, pp. 54-56.

Hugo, Graeme (1998). "The demographic underpinnings of current and future international migration in Asia", *Asian and Pacific Migration Journal*, vol. 7, No. 1, pp. 1-25.

Hui, Weng-Tat (1998). "The regional economic crisis and Singapore: Implications for labor migration", *Asian and Pacific Migration Journal*, vol. 7, Nos. 2-3.

Hui, Weng-Tat (2001). "Foreign manpower and development strategy in Singapore", in *Proceedings of the International Workshop on International Migration and Structural Change in the APEC Member Economies*, compiled by Yasuko Hayase and Ching-lung Tsay, (Chiba, Japan, IDE – JETRO).

International Monetary Fund (IMF) (2001). *World Economic Outlook: May 2001*, (Washington DC, IMF).

International Organization for Migration (IOM) (1999). "Overview of the current situation of irregular or undocumented migration in the East and Southeast Asian region: The need for a policy response framework", paper presented at the International Symposium on Migration "Toward Regional Cooperation on Irregular/Undocumented Migration," Bangkok, 21-23 April.

International Organization for Migration (IOM) (2000a). *World Migration Report 2000*, (IOM and United Nations).

31

International Organization for Migration (IOM) (2000b). "Trafficking in children in Southeast Asia", *Asian Migrant*, vol. 13, No. 2, pp. 52-64.

Iredale, Robyn (2000). "Migration policies for the highly-skilled in the Asia-Pacific region", *International Migration Review*, vol. 34, pp. 882-906.

Kanapathy, Vijayakumari (2001). "International migration and labour market adjustment in Malaysia: The role of foreign labor management policies", *Asian and Pacific Migration Journal,* vol. 14, Nos. 3-4, pp. 429-462.

Lebedev, Mikhail (1999). "Some experiences of the Commonwealth of Independent States in combating irregular/undocumented migration", *Asian Migrant*, vol. 12, No. 3.

Massey, Douglas and others (1998). *Worlds in Motion: Understanding International Migration at the End of the Millennium,* (Oxford, Clarendon Press).

Organisation for Economic Co-operation and Development (OECD) SOPEMI (1998). *Trends in International Migration: Annual Report,* (Paris, OECD).

Prasad, Bishnu (2000). "Nepal", in, Raghwan and Michal Sebastian (eds.), *ILO Asia Pacific Regional Trade Union Symposium on Migrant Workers, 6-8 December 1999*, (Geneva, Bureau for Workers Activities and International Labour Office).

Robles, Alan and Sanjay Kapoor (2001). "Brain power", *Asiaweek,* 18 May.

Rowlands, Dane (1998). "Poverty and environmental degradation as root causes of international migration: A critical assessment", paper presented at the Technical Symposium on International Migration and Development, The Hague, 29 June - 3 July.

Saith, A. (1997). *Migration Pressures and Structural Change: Case Study of the Philippines,* International Migration Papers No.19, (Geneva, International Labour Office).

Saraswati, Muninggar (2001). "Are women sold cheaper than goats?" *Jakarta Post,* 5 November.

Scalabrini Migration Center (SMC) (2001). *Asian Migration Atlas, <http:// www.scalabrini.asn.au/amatlas/amatlas.htm>.*

Sheehan, Deidre (2001). "Praying for Christmas", *Far Eastern Economic Review*, 8 November.

Skeldon, Ronald (2000). "Trafficking: A perspective from Asia", *International Migration*, vol. 38, No. 3, pp. 7-30.

SyCip, Ly, Maruja Asis and Emmanuel Luna (2000). *The Measurement of Filipino Well-Being,* (Diliman, Philippines, University of the Philippines).

Tsay, Ching-lung and Ji-ping Lin (2001). "Labour importation and unemployment in Taiwan", *Asian and Pacific Migration Journal,* vol. 10, Nos. 3-4, pp. 505-534.

United Nations (2000). "The UN Population Division on replacement migration", *Population and Development Review*, vol. 26, No. 2, pp. 413-417.

Wong, Diana (1997). "Transience and settlement: Singapore's foreign labor policy", *Asian and Pacific Migration Journal*, vol. 6, No. 2.

# CHAPTER II

## MIGRATION IN PACIFIC ISLAND COUNTRIES AND TERRITORIES

By John Connell[*]

In the island microstates of the South Pacific, the prospects for economic growth are unusually limited. The currently widely perceived disparities in economic development and welfare between the Pacific States, especially the smallest countries and territories of Polynesia and Micronesia, and the fringing metropolitan countries, have contributed not only to substantial migration but also to increasing pressures for further international migration. Almost all of that migration has occurred since the 1960s. As emigration continues, small and vulnerable South Pacific States have become irrevocably a peripheral and dependent part of a wider world. Contemporary patterns of migration have diversified, demographic structures have changed and the restructuring of global and island economic landscapes present different development contexts. Essentially the life courses of island people, present or absent, are increasingly embedded in international ties. Much of the largest migration streams have been from Polynesia, notably Samoa and Tonga, while there is currently increasingly rapid migration from the independent Micronesian States that were once linked closely to the United States of America.

The variety of reasons put forward to explain migration in the South Pacific sometimes seems interminable and the problems of generalization considerable. Apart from migration as a result of natural hazards, the major influences are economic, even where social changes are also significant. Migration is primarily a response to real and perceived inequalities in socio-economic opportunities that are themselves a result of dependent and/or uneven sectoral and regional

---

[*] Professor of Geography and Head, School of Geosciences, University of Sydney, Australia.

development. Social influences on migration are important, especially in terms of access to education and health services, but also as one element of the transition to adulthood; such social influences are in turn often a function of economic issues. Migration remains, in different forms, a time-honoured strategy of moving from a poor area to a richer one in the search for social and economic mobility at home or abroad.

A major influence on migration has been radical changes in expectations over what constitutes a satisfactory standard of living, a desirable occupation and a suitable mix of accessible services and amenities. In parallel with changing aspirations and the increased necessity to earn cash, agricultural work throughout the Pacific has been losing prestige, and the relatively limited and declining participation of young men in the agricultural economy is ubiquitous. Changes in values, following increased educational opportunities and the expansion of bureaucratic (largely urban) employment within the region in the 1970s, have further oriented migration streams away from the region, as local employment opportunities have not kept pace with population growth. This situation continued throughout the 1990s. The resultant changes have also contributed to the widening gap between expectations, which are themselves continually being revised upward, and the reality of limited domestic employment and incomes.

International movements have been paralleled by intensified migration within particular countries. This migration has been characterized by movement away from remote islands and isolated rural areas, to more accessible coastal locations and particularly to urban areas, which have grown considerably in recent years. Thus, national populations have become increasingly concentrated on the more central, urbanized islands such as Tongatapu in Tonga, Upolu in Samoa, South Tarawa in Kiribati and Efate in Vanuatu. This has tended to accentuate problems of service delivery in remote areas. This situation has in turn accentuated and accounted for some of that movement away from isolated areas.

# THE MIGRATION ENVIRONMENT

## The socio-economic context

As in other small economies, development in island States is constrained by the limits of small size. Well-known influences include: remoteness and isolation (resulting in high transport costs to markets); diseconomies of scale (because of small domestic markets); limited natural resources and a narrow production base, substantial trade deficits (because of dependency on metropolitan States); few local skills; vulnerability to external shocks and natural disasters; and a disproportionately high expenditure on administration and dependence on external institutions (such as banks and universities) for some key services. Moreover, political systems have sometimes been fragile, ecological structures are vulnerable and economies lack diversity. Small islands, a paucity of natural resources and remoteness, even within countries and territories, have hampered the ability of such States to compete in the global economy. Consequently, island economies have traditionally specialized in a very narrow range of agricultural exports, such as copra and coffee. Export diversity in the Pacific subregion is less than in any other world region. Set against this range of disadvantages, the comparative advantages of smallness and isolation are few, other than the retention of a degree of cultural integrity (Connell, 1988). Although the subregion does not suffer the absolute depths of poverty experienced in some parts of the developing world, it does have serious social and economic problems. Economic growth has been disappointing since independence, expanding populations have intensified pressure on lands and seas, and political instability has increased.

Most countries, other than Melanesian States, have benefited from aid flows and remittances, enabling them to run big current account deficits, maintain substantial bureaucracies and undertake relatively large public sector investment programmes of a kind that could not otherwise be financed. The Pacific islands are the most heavily aid-assisted part of the world on a per capita basis. The public sector dominates formal economic activity everywhere and, despite the availability of external resources and sound financial management, national incomes have largely stagnated since the 1980s.

In some contexts in the subregion, international migration has been viewed as a kind of "safety-valve", reducing pressures on national Governments to provide employment opportunities and welfare services, especially in conditions of high rates of natural population increase and low rates of economic growth. There is little evidence so far that the safety-valve of international migration enabled sending countries to gain significantly from a reduction in domestic population and/or to have benefited from the receipt of remittances to restructure their economies. Migration has tended to be viewed as a substitute for development rather than as a short-term support for increasing the effectiveness of national development efforts.

Migration decisions are often shaped within a family context; that is, they are rarely individualistic. Migrants leave to meet certain family expectations, one of

37

which is financial support for kin. Greater ease of migration and a growing familiarity with external affairs have contributed to an increase in individual – rather than family or lineage – decision-making, but these expectations remain valid. Overall, migration is directed at improving both the living standards of those who remain at home and the lifestyle and income of the migrants. More specifically, in rural areas and home islands, as in Tonga, "migration and remittances . . . are perceived solely as means for improving family incomes and welfare rather than for direct or indirect national economic development" (Tongamoa, 1987, p. 67). Migration has rarely been an individual decision to meet individual goals, nor has it been dictated by national interests (except perhaps in the case of Kiribati and Tuvalu).

The underlying economic rationale of migration is reflected in its household organization extending to a world stage. Bertram (1985) has suggested that Tongan (and other similar) households are characterized "by remittance transfers among various component parts of the 'transnational corporations of kin' which direct the allocation of each island's family labour around the regional economy". Consequently, "families deliberate carefully about which members would be most likely to do well overseas and be reliable in sending remittances" (Gailey, 1992, p. 465; Cowling, 1990).

## Population change

The onset of the demographic transition in the Pacific has been preceded by a period of rapidly increasing fertility. In the western Melanesian States, that period is still under way; Solomon Islands has a population growth rate of around 3.4 per cent and Vanuatu around 2.6 per cent. Growth rates are also high in Micronesia. In the Polynesian States and Fiji, the growth rates that caused alarm in the 1950s and 1960s have fallen, less because of lowered fertility than because of emigration, a "safety valve" for continued high fertility rates (table 1).

Total fertility rates (TFR) are very high in several countries and territories. In Solomon Islands and Vanuatu, TFRs have only just fallen below 6 children per woman. In Polynesia, they are somewhat lower; with the exceptions of Fiji and Palau, all the island States have rates above the mean of 2.5 for the ESCAP region. Fertility rates are high since contraceptive use is low, particularly compared with the situation that exists in other developing countries of similar income levels. Fertility control is a taboo topic in public discussions in most countries. Throughout the region, there is no indication that contraceptive use rates are anywhere above 30 per cent; they may be as low as 3 to 4 per cent in

38

Vanuatu and Solomon Islands. Many reasons explain the limited response to family planning, including the availability of children to perform work (especially in their parents' old age), children's potential to be income-earners, the desire and necessity to please husbands, the intrinsic need to produce and rear children, and the limited access to family planning services.

**Table 1. Selected demographic characteristics for Pacific island countries and territories, 2001**

| Country or territory and region | Mid-2001 population (thousands) | Annual growth rate (percentage) | Total fertility rate (children per woman) | Urban population | |
|---|---|---|---|---|---|
| | | | | Percentage urban (2001) | Annual growth rate (%) |
| Pacific | 31 046 | 1.4 | 2.3 | 70 | 1.2 |
| American Samoa | 66 | 2.9 | .. | 53 | 4.4 |
| Australia | 19 388 | 1.2 | 1.8 | 85 | 1.0 |
| Cook Islands | 19 | -0.5 | 3.7 | 60 | 1.0 |
| Fiji | 823 | 1.1 | 3.1 | 50 | 2.9 |
| French Polynesia | 237 | 1.6 | 2.5 | 53 | 1.4 |
| Guam | 158 | 1.9 | 4.0 | 40 | 2.5 |
| Kiribati | 93 | 2.5 | 4.5 | 40 | 2.7 |
| Marshall Islands | 53 | 2.0 | .. | 72 | 3.8 |
| Micronesia (Federated States of) | 120 | 1.9 | .. | 29 | 3.1 |
| Nauru | 12 | 1.8 | .. | 100 | 1.8 |
| New Caledonia | 220 | 2.0 | 2.5 | 78 | 3.2 |
| New Zealand | 3 901 | 0.8 | 1.9 | 86 | 1.1 |
| Niue | 2 | -3.1 | .. | 33 | -0.7 |
| Northern Mariana Islands | 81 | 5.5 | 2.1 | 53 | 5.6 |
| Palau | 20 | 2.2 | .. | 73 | 2.7 |
| Papua New Guinea | 4 920 | 2.3 | 4.4 | 18 | 4.0 |
| Samoa | 159 | 0.3 | 4.3 | 22 | 2.6 |
| Solomon Islands | 463 | 3.4 | 5.4 | 20 | 5.8 |
| Tonga | 101 | 0.6 | 4.2 | 39 | 1.8 |
| Tuvalu | 10 | 0.9 | .. | 53 | 4.5 |
| Vanuatu | 202 | 2.6 | 4.4 | 20 | 3.9 |

*Source: 2001 ESCAP Population Data Sheet,* (Bangkok, United Nations Economic and Social Commission for Asia and the Pacific).

Throughout the Pacific, life expectancies have risen over the past quarter of a century. Crude birth rates are low, though these are partly a function of a youthful age structure. In several states, the rates by the end of the 1980s were 5 per 1,000, but in the Melanesian States (other than Fiji) they were at least twice that level. Life expectancies are lower in the Melanesian States (for example, in Papua New Guinea, life expectancy is no more than 57 years), whereas the Polynesian States have life expectancies higher than 65 years. Infant mortality rates are rather similar in structure, with Kiribati and Papua New Guinea again being the worst in the subregion, and infant mortality is worsening in Papua New Guinea. Most countries, but especially those of Melanesia, are only entering the early phases of the demographic transition.

The extent to which population pressure on resources has been perceived as a problem is extremely variable. Concerns were first raised among and about coral atoll populations. In Kiribati and Tuvalu, this was apparent by the mid-nineteenth century; as early as 1865, it was suggested that the local people "were the first genuine Malthusians. They feared that unless the population was kept down they would not have sufficient food" (cited by Munro and Bedford, 1980, p. 3). By the 1890s, resettlement was already being suggested as a solution to what was perceived as an impending overpopulation problem. In the 1940s, resettlement on a small scale had become a reality, with the migration of Vaitupu islanders to Kioa, a Fijian island, purchased by the colonial administration. Elsewhere in Polynesia there was little concern for growing populations, until well into the twentieth century. However, in the 1960s the United Nations drew attention to rapid population growth in Samoa, and both there and in Tonga, the first significant international migration began. Throughout Melanesia, indigenous responses to population growth are viewed in terms of migration, rather than direct controls on population growth.

Although prolonged rural-to-urban migration, increasing pressure on both rural land and urban services, rising youth unemployment, social discontent and high levels of maternal mortality all contributed to a more favourable climate for establishing population policies in Papua New Guinea (McMurray, 1992, p. 13) as elsewhere in Melanesia, achieving policy targets has proved impossible. The factors that are most conducive to successful population policies – integration of population and development policies, improved rural development and communications to spread new values and reduce the economic significance of children, formal-sector employment opportunities for women of increasing age at marriage – are largely absent. In some places, including Tuvalu, the possibility of migration has actually encouraged high rates of natural increase; at the household level, on Nanumea atoll, "parents actively hope to produce remittance earners and most feel that this necessitates having more than one son [one of whom] will be our road to money and imported goods" (Chambers, 1986, pp. 283-284). Despite the failures of family planning, the most rapid phase of population growth in the Pacific is probably over now, even though growth rates remain high. The outcome has been that in most States there is a preponderance of young adults in the population, a situation that has placed strains on land resources, but also on employment markets, education and social organization. A critical development issue throughout the Pacific is that of maintaining – let alone improving – current standards of living in the face of rapid population increases.

# CONTEMPORARY MIGRATIONS

The 22 States that comprise the Pacific island countries and territories are traditionally aggregated into three major indigenous groups: Polynesia, Micronesia and Melanesia. These three groupings are characterized by quite distinct mixes of international and internal migration patterns, with Polynesia being a major point of origin of international migrants, Melanesia a place of intense internal flows and Micronesia a combination of both.

According to the International Organization for Migration (IOM and United Nations, 2000), approximately 400,000 people of Pacific island ethnicity lived abroad in the mid-1990s. While not very significant relative to the Pacific island population as a whole (around 6 million), these figures are highly significant for the small countries and territories of Polynesia and Micronesia. For instance, emigrants account for 75 per cent of the Polynesian population; and 30 to 40 per cent of the population of Samoa and Tonga are estimated to be living abroad. Most of these international migrants are in New Zealand (170,000), where the three Pacific island countries of Samoa, Fiji and Tonga were in the top 10

**Table 2. Pacific islanders approved for residence in New Zealand from the periods 1992/93 to 1997/98**

| Country | 1992/93 | 1993/94 | 1994/95 | 1995/96 | 1996/97 | 1997/98 | Total | Percentage |
|---------|---------|---------|---------|---------|---------|---------|-------|------------|
| Samoa | 1,482 | 983 | 1,525 | 2,282 | 2,387 | 1,835 | 10,494 | 5 |
| Fiji | 905 | 704 | 920 | 1,067 | 1,422 | 1,746 | 6,764 | 3 |
| Tonga | 1,367 | 587 | 871 | 798 | 949 | 932 | 5,504 | 2 |

*Source : World Migration Report: 2000,* (Geneva, International Organization for Migration and United Nations, 2000).

41

countries of origin between 1992 and 1997, accounting respectively for 5, 3 and 2 per cent of total immigration to New Zealand (table 2). Significant numbers were also found in the United States (145,000), in Australia (84,000) and Canada (16,700).

## International migration from the Pacific islands

### Polynesia

International migration to the metropolitan countries and territories on the fringes of the Pacific is primarily a Polynesian phenomenon. Many people from American Samoa, Cook Islands, Niue, Samoa and Tonga have moved either to New Zealand (whence some have gone on to Australia) or, increasingly, to the United States as the New Zealand economy has stagnated and immigration restrictions have become tighter. For the smallest States, including Cook Islands, Niue, Pitcairn and Tokelau, migration has been particularly dramatic since the majority of the ethnic population live overseas.

Samoa and Tonga share a history of substantial emigration lasting for more than three decades; in each of the Polynesian States, population growth and urbanization have been slowed by emigration, not least because of the loss of the most fertile groups. Though both Samoa and Tonga experienced some emigration in the early post-war years, large-scale movements effectively began in the late 1960s. A combination of reasons, including recognition of substantial income differentials between Polynesia and metropolitan countries such as New Zealand and the United States, increased expectations of superior education and health services, improved transport links (especially air transport), a relative reduction in transport costs and growing population pressure on domestic resources, all stimulated mobility. In the early 1980s, migration slowed because of adverse economic conditions in New Zealand and migration streams increasingly shifted towards the United States, often via American Samoa (Ahlburg and Levin, 1990). Current estimates suggest that almost as many Samoans and Tongans live overseas as at home, in countries where their future is intricately related to economic prosperity, recession, restructuring and the nature of the employment market. At no time during the previous quarter of a century has there been substantial return migration; moreover, in Samoa prospects for emigration were so poor at the start of the 1980s that the "broken dreams" of potential migrants contributed to a significant rise in youth suicide (Macpherson and Macpherson, 1987). At the national level, the economic future of the two States partly hinges on the continued flow of remittances, and hence on some continuity of migration

(Ahlburg, 1991; Connell and Brown, 1995). The possibility of blocked migration in the future, a situation ever present in public debate (Macpherson, 1992; Shankman, 1993), emphasizes the potential problem of a high rate of natural increase in case emigration is substantially reduced, since there is now a "culture of migration": emigration is normal, expected and anticipated, and it is an important element in national social and economic systems.

## Micronesia

The former United States territories of Micronesia – Marshall Islands, Palau and particularly the Federated States of Micronesia – have increasingly exhibited similar trends. For even longer, Kiribati and Tuvalu have been characterized by migration, but of contract labour – mainly to Nauru (for employment in the phosphate mine) or to work in the international shipping industry (for which both countries have training schools) – hence return migration is normal, and the impact on national population change is less significant.

Kiribati and Tuvalu are rather different, despite labour migration for more than a century. Though Tuvalu has experienced relatively little permanent emigration, in 1991 there were more than 1,200 Tuvaluans overseas, more than 10 per cent of the national population. The largest number of these (735) were on Nauru where the phosphate workings were reaching the end of their life, ultimately necessitating the return of these contract workers to Tuvalu. In Kiribati, where there were some 3,000 I-Kiribati overseas in the mid-1990s, the situation is almost identical to that in Tuvalu. Kiribati and Tuvalu are two of the very few countries in the world where the local population is trained for work overseas; however, the future of overseas migrants – as seamen, miners, students or contract workers in New Zealand – is insecure. Both countries face the more inevitable and perhaps more imminent return of a very significant proportion of their population.

The signing of the Compacts of Free Association, giving Micronesians unrestricted access to the United States, quickly encouraged movement by some of those with skills who could not find government employment at home, led students to seek permanent residence in the United States, and stimulated rapid migration by the Chuukese (Federated States of Micronesia), in particular, to Guam and Saipan. A more comprehensive pattern of international movement accelerated and spread in the 1990s (Hezel and Levin, 1996). Overall, more than 10,000 citizens of the Federated States of Micronesia may be currently outside the country. A broadly similar situation is also true of Palau, though it has been established much longer, and Marshall Islands (Smith, 1996; Ogden, 1994, pp.

43

256-260) where emigration has been particularly rapid in the 1990s. The migration process in Micronesia is becoming increasingly similar to that in other parts of the South Pacific: a steady outflow, growth of relatively permanent urban communities overseas (beyond student groups) and the compensatory flow of remittances. As elsewhere, a culture of migration has gradually become established.

In rather different ways, the future of each of the Polynesian and Micronesian States is bound up with the present and the future of international migration and the ability of these countries and territories to seek new potential destinations overseas. All have retained interest in overseas employment opportunities. Both Kiribati and Tuvalu have experienced resettlement overseas, and Tonga has leased agricultural land in Asia. In the 1980s, the Jackson Committee on Australian Foreign Aid recommended that special provision be made for migration from Kiribati and Tuvalu because of the improbability of conventional aid contributing to sustainable national development. More recently, Tuvalu's Prime Minister emphasized that his country was continuing to seek employment and migration opportunities in Australia and that Tuvalu "would not take no for an answer" on the provision of either employment or educational opportunities, regarded as necessary for economic survival and potentially critical in the face of a possible rise in the sea level in the future (Connell, 1999). Rising material consumption levels following migration have generated increased demand for consumer goods, a demand that can be satisfied only by further migration, as migrants bypass the small towns of the Pacific to seek superior living conditions overseas.

## Melanesia

In the larger countries of Melanesia, economies have been more viable, political ties less effective and emigration conspicuous by its absence, though there has been significant emigration from Fiji, especially of Indo-Fijians. This dramatically accelerated after the 1987 and 2000 coups d'état, with migration to Australia and New Zealand as well as Canada.

### Skilled migration

There is a general unwillingness on the part of both sending and receiving countries to acknowledge the flows of skilled labour in and around the Pacific subregion (Iredale, 2000), but there is some indication that skilled workers in general, and medical workers in particular, make up a higher proportion of immigrants from island States to metropolitan States because of the increased focus on skilled migration (within declining immigration numbers) in most destinations, and the continued (and increasing) demand for health workers there (see below). Each of the principal destinations for skilled migrants – Australia, Canada, New Zealand and the United States – has the acquisition of permanent skilled migrants as one of the objectives of its immigration policies. Indeed they have become competitors in trying to attract highly skilled (and entrepreneurial) migrants (Cobb-Clark and Connelly, 1997). Ironically, many of those migrants become part of a "brain loss" or "brain-waste" because their qualifications, despite contributing to gaining them entry, are unrecognized in the destination country.

In some small States, the brain drain has been excessive: Cook Islands, for example, lost more than half its vocationally qualified population in the single decade 1966-1976 (Cook Islands, 1984, p. 23) and much the same happened again in the mid-1990s when the national economy collapsed. In the case of the migration of Samoans and Tongans to the United States alone, "Emigration results in the permanent loss of young educated skilled labour from the Pacific island nations. Skilled labour is in short supply and emigration probably hinders development" (Ahlburg and Levin, 1990, p. 84). This is certainly true more generally in the health sector, where more costly (and sometimes less skilled) replacements have sometimes been required, and in the movement of sportsmen. It is widely true within the government sector in Samoa (Liki, 1994) and almost certainly evident elsewhere. Moreover, skilled migrants are more easily and more likely to migrate following political or other problems, as was the case in Fiji in both 1987 and 2000. The combination of changing aspirations and the migration of the more educated young contributes to the brain and skill drain from national peripheries and from small States, perhaps ultimately worsening the welfare and bargaining position of those places (Connell, 2001).

Few studies of return migration in the Pacific have been undertaken, partly because the volume of return migration is small relative to the outward flow. The limited early evidence available suggested that this was dominated by the retired or by "failures". However, that may disguise some degree of return migration of the relatively skilled (Liki, 1994) and, at the very least, return migration across a wide range of categories (Maron, 2001). Many skilled, qualified and experienced people from Cook Islands have returned to the islands and have been able to use their skills in a range of occupations, not merely in the public service (Hooker and Varcoe, 1999, p. 96). Cook Islands is unusual, however, in that wages and salaries in the islands are somewhat comparable with those in the destination country.

The limited extent of return migration is at least partly due to the great differences in income levels between the island Pacific and the metropolitan periphery. It is a function of the situation where the children of migrants are educated in the destination country and have lost some degree of contact with "home" societies even to the extent where they have lost critical linguistic and other skills. This is also linked to a gradual shift in the demographic balance, especially in the Polynesian States, from those States to the metropolitan fringe; relatives are increasingly likely to be found in the destination countries.

In small island States, it is unusually difficult to replace skilled migrants, both because of the duration of training that is required and the very small demand for some particular skills. This is again particularly true of highly skilled health workers. Although this is less true for nurses and doctors, since their numbers are rather larger, it is even more true of the smallest island States. It is equally evident that, because of the necessity for appropriate skill training, it is more difficult to substitute for absent skills in the health workforce – or transfer them from elsewhere in the public service. The outcome is that basic needs are less well provided, especially in remote areas or outer islands, and large proportions of budgets are directed to referrals to distant places.

## Internal migration

The depopulation of small islands and remote mountainous areas is widespread in the Pacific. Employment opportunities and services (especially education) are concentrated in the urban centres and on small island States. Where manpower and capital are often limited, centralization is inevitable at some scale. The more educated have tended to migrate first and migrants have left many rural areas to take advantage of superior urban educational and employment opportunities. As in Palau, educational systems create disdain for rural life because "the exclusion of traditional skills and knowledge from westernized school curricula in many developing countries amounts to a constant tacit assumption that such things are not worth learning" (Johannes, 1981, p. 148). In the squatter settlement of Blacksands (Port Vila, Vanuatu), around 7 per cent of families had moved there for a better education for their children. Yet, though many had achieved it, some were forced to send their children back to the village for education, as urban schools became full. A few families dismissed education, believing it no longer offered a guarantee of employment or the opportunity to improve living standards. Such families were usually financially disadvantaged and with little education (Mecartney, 2001); hence, the restricted access to education for their children was likely to perpetuate and accentuate the structure of uneven development. More recently, and primarily in parts of Papua New Guinea (Connell, 1997), there are growing indications that migrants have moved away from inadequate rural opportunities, not because of the perceived superiority of urban opportunities, but out of increasing rural impoverishment.

Migration is principally a response to real and perceived spatial inequalities in socio-economic opportunities. Though urban areas display high levels of open unemployment, migration continues because differentials between urban and rural average incomes remain substantial; thus, migration hampers both economic growth and development. In most countries, earning power is increasingly concentrated among urban bureaucracies while the absence of developed State mechanisms (such as progressive taxation, unemployment benefits and pension schemes) for affecting transfers of income, minimizes redistribution towards rural areas other than through personal remittances. Yet, an economic rationale, real or latent, ultimately underlies most migration moves. In the squatter settlements of Blacksands, in Port Vila, and Ivane, in Port Moresby (Papua New Guinea), most migrants arrived for employment, and others for the superior education that might secure them a good job in the future (Mecartney, 2001; Vavine, 1984). Simply stated, in Port Vila, one of the most important reasons was "*long winem smal vatu from no gat rod long winim vatu long aelan* (to earn a little money since there's no way to earn money on the home island)" (Mitchell, 2000, p. 172). For many, that is reason enough. Growing inequalities, coupled with rising expectations, are the concomitants of increased migration.

Especially in the post-independence era, the number of white-collar and similarly prestigious occupations has increased considerably, especially in urban areas. The expansion of education has trained more people to be able to take such jobs, and opportunities (however limited) are available to the young that had only exceptionally been available to their parents. Expectations are steadily rising but, at the same time, employment crises in many urban areas, growing rural populations, inflation, static (or even falling) commodity prices and the declining availability of land in some areas slowly increase the gap between expectations and reality. This increasing gap is one of the critical problems of development in the region.

Tertiary education is usually undertaken outside the home island, especially in the smaller States, further contributing to emigration. The Tongan anthropologist, Epeli Hau'ofa, has summarized the situation succinctly: "Once you are educated, once your mind is expanded, subsistence on a remote little island is simply unacceptable.... Psychologically we are no longer islanders" (quoted by Dyson, 1982, p. 120). Consequently, "migrants seek in the West access to material goods,

47

jobs in the industrial sector, better education for their young, and social mobility in a society they have believed free of the traditional barriers of rank and family status that made such mobility difficult at home" (Shore, 1978, p. xiii). Experience and perceptions of the wider world, its values, and its material rewards further underlie the migratory experience. Migration of the young to Koror has been summed up by one Palauan as the three Es: "employment, entertainment and education" (Rehuher, 1993, p. 21) – a not uncommon situation.

The existence of kin in urban areas is a major influence and support. Not only do they provide demonstrations, or create images, of an impressive lifestyle, they may also provide remittances (the visible monetary symbols of success), fares and accommodation for new migrants to the city. Many who initially visit towns for education or health reasons just stay on with relatives. Because of these kinds of explanations and justifications, and the post-facto rationalization of decision-making, migration is often best seen "as an almost inevitable decision that they [villagers] will have to make sooner or later and once this view is accepted a sort of migration momentum develops" (Walsh, 1982, p. 7). This stimulates chain migration; in many contexts, it appears to be a chain reaction. Rising expectations in the wake of independence and growing materialism have exacerbated the shift from production to consumption, the decline of exchange and an increase in social tensions. The spreading taste for commodities has influenced work habits, and, for many in the Pacific, the largest cities and the metropolitan countries exercise a powerful allure, offer a sense of future, and simply validate migration.

## Urbanization

Accelerated migration in the 1970s brought about rapid urbanization, the growth of squatter settlements and the early recognition of urban development problems. A growing differentiation has emerged between those permanent urban residents who are relatively poor (including some long-established urban villagers and the migrants from poor rural areas) and others who are well off. This became most apparent in Melanesia and, to a lesser extent, Micronesia. Those who were particularly disadvantaged had little or no support from the rural economy and no opportunity to move away from town when poverty, rising unemployment, old age or social disorder made urban life difficult, at least for those who were, in one way or another, "trapped" in town. In Blacksands, insecurity over land tenure and employment ensured that migrants contemplated return, but most believed they would remain in town for their children's sake (Mecartney, 2001, p. 80). The combination of growing urban permanency, high unemployment and increased expectations have put considerable pressure on urban services.

The benefits of migration to urban areas were particularly apparent in the early post-war decades when migration and urbanization were assumed to be concomitants of economic growth and development. Migration enabled individuals to obtain higher education and technical training (or merely gain experience in a different milieu) and contribute to urban and national development through their labour. Many new skills were also of value elsewhere, in the event of return migration. Not only did migration have positive benefits in the towns but it also contributed both to a reduction in population pressure on resources in rural areas and to natural resource development (usually in mines and plantations) elsewhere. Consequently, until recently, urbanization in the Pacific was viewed positively. In Papua New Guinea, where urbanization was relatively late, towns on the eve of independence were seen as centres of national social, economic and political development. There were then few urban problems and no real hostility to urbanization in the subregion.

Over time, attitudes to urbanization hardened, through prejudice against squatter settlements rather than any notion of rural development policy. Squatter settlements are widely perceived to be haunts of the feckless unemployed (though there is little evidence of this being particularly prevalent); a significant proportion of employment is in the informal sector and this is rarely regarded as appropriate or genuine employment. A correlation between urban crime levels and recent migration is frequently voiced but also lacks demonstrable proof; there is no evidence that crime levels, or gang membership, are more obviously correlated with settlement residence (Goddard, 1992; 2001; Nibbrig, 1992). It is not implausible however that social disorganization and crime are a function of substantial inequalities in access to land, housing and other services in the largest cities. Certainly some Papua New Guinea criminals themselves have pointed to crime being a response to both inequalities and their perceptions of corruption and other "white collar" offences that have gone unpunished. Crime tends to exacerbate the deprivation experienced in settlements, and to make them a source of greater concern among other urban residents.

In Papua New Guinea especially, opposition to urbanization has continued from both urban authorities and influential leaders. For example, in mid-1991 the Morobe Premier sought to eject all illegal settlers from the coastal city of Lae: "My plan to eject settlers is a genuine one for the sake of my people who want a trouble free environment for their children .... As for Papua New Guinea which has a large area of land, I do not see why people should move from province to province. I am sure there are better things to do in their own villages or towns" (*TPNG*, 6 June 1991). Not surprisingly these were not the settlers'

49

perceptions. Similar policies there and in other Papua New Guinea towns, especially the largest ones, have continued throughout the decade (Connell and Lea, 2002; Goddard, 2001; Koczberski and others, 2001) in the guise of achieving order and cleanliness, reducing crime and unemployment, freeing land for business development, and demonstrating that the State was not weak. Destruction and violence – against settlements – have become instruments of urban planning as urban problems become increasingly complex and unmanageable.

In Vanuatu too, settlements in official discourses and newspapers have also been seen as places of "squatters" and sources of criminals, "a blight in paradise and a place of transgression", from where people should return home (Mitchell, 2000, p. 192) but no direct action has been taken. Settlements, unemployment and crime are discursively linked by politicians, police spokespersons and "monotonously repeated in the daily press", or on radio stations, alongside routine conceptualizations about the inevitable consequences of urban migration and poverty (Goddard, 2001, p. 4) that invariably lack substance. At the very least there is a considerable diversity of settlements and settlers, though the claims of settlers for financial support, through service schemes and social amenity provision, are unlikely to be met – except at election times – and are usually routinely rejected. Such intermittent ambivalence and weak governance has meant that, even though there has been an enormous amount of debate, it has not been possible anywhere to formulate an effective policy to discourage or remove (or even upgrade) squatter settlements. In contrast to the widespread opposition to urbanization – at least in the form of settlements – there has been minimal support for the rights of settlement residents, other than from themselves. Meanwhile, the pervasive opposition to urbanization has delayed and discouraged the development of coordinated plans for urban management, and hence the reduction of urban development problems.

## MIGRATION, POVERTY AND DEVELOPMENT

### The role of remittances

In very diverse migration contexts, an economic rationale is significant and remittances play an important role, especially where migration is from small island States, or from small islands in larger Pacific States such as Papua New Guinea. In many countries and territories, remittances form a significant part of disposable income, so much so that the smaller island States (specifically initially Cook Islands, Kiribati, Tokelau and Tuvalu) have been conceptualized as

"MIRAB States," where Migration, Remittances, Aid and the resultant (largely urban) Bureaucracy are central to the socio-economic system (Bertram and Watters, 1985). While this acronym is disliked in the Pacific because of its implication of a "handout mentality", it nonetheless suggests the centrality of migration and remittances in the island States, and has been largely unchallenged for two decades (Bertram, 1999). Moreover, it has spawned other acronyms such as MURAB, which places extra and appropriate emphasis on the attendant urbanization within island States such as Tuvalu (Munro, 1990), and even MIAB, where migration has not stimulated a significant flow of remittances, as in some parts of Micronesia (Ogden, 1994; Karakita, 1997).

In Tonga, migrants have been seen as part of a "transnational corporation of kin", who may seek to maximize extended household incomes across different continents (Marcus, 1981), and in so doing not only help to maintain these family and communal networks, but may also even enlarge their social fields of interaction, incorporating them into multilocal networks of support and empowerment. Remittances have raised living standards, contributed to employment (especially in the service and construction sectors) and eased balance of payments problems, despite contributing to inflation, especially in the larger Polynesian countries. However, increased demand for improved consumer goods can usually be met only by further migration, and it has generally been argued that little of the remittances has been invested in economic growth.

While macroeconomic data suggest that remittances have not led to increased inter-household income inequality within Tonga (Ahlburg, 1991), village-level studies have demonstrated considerable income inequality (Hardaker and others, 1987) and suggested that this is partly a result of remittance flows (Gailey, 1992; Small, 1997, pp. 134, 195). It is certainly a widespread perception in most island States. Marcus (1993, pp. 29-30) has thus suggested, again almost a decade ago, that "the capacity to call on international resources has become a crucial factor in influencing a family's local economic conditions". People in the lowest stratum in contemporary Tonga are those totally dependent on the nation-state framework, and the limited resources it embodies, without any overseas options at all. Indeed it is increasingly argued that "every family needs to have someone overseas. Otherwise the family is to be pitied" (quoted in Small, 1997, p. 152); hence, in contrast to western societies, it is often the single-female-headed households that survive most effectively (Gailey, 1992). In this kind of situation, in Tonga, perhaps to a greater extent than anywhere else in the Pacific, the migration-remittance nexus has become very firmly established. Demand for migration and remittances is likely to be sustained, alongside rising expectations in conditions of limited national economic growth.

Because of the continued significance of remittances, the sustainability of remittance-dependent development is particularly important – and somewhat uncertain – because the need of the countries of origin for remittances is likely to grow faster than its supply. The rate of growth of migration to major destinations, namely, Australia, New Zealand and the United States, has declined in recent years owing to economic recession in the destination countries, and the restructuring of migration controls. Though incomes from outside the islands (whether remittances or aid) have tended to contribute to inflation and raise the shadow price of labour, and thus may have depressed some local development activities, they have allowed for higher material standards of living in small countries and islands where the local resource base would otherwise set constraints to many development objectives.

### The urban informal sector: opportunities for rural migrants?

In still primarily subsistence-oriented economies, employment is essentially an urban phenomenon. It is usually considered to be worse in the informal settlements, especially those of recent origin, yet what Jackson (1976, p. 49) recorded of Papua New Guinea towns a quarter of a century ago remains true: "settlements are frequently the homes of people less transitory, no more unemployed and just as urbanized as other sectors of the population". In the Blacksands settlement of Port Vila, for instance, most people were employed in the city, including in senior government positions, alongside work in the private sector or as Christian pastors. The service sector dominated employment through drivers, domestic workers, construction workers, gardeners or shops assistants; increasingly, women took on "non-traditional" roles, such as working in stores, and became the main income earners in some households. Employment was linked to skills (and age) rather than kinship ties. The broad structure of employment in the settlement was similar to that in Port Vila as a whole (Mecartney, 2001).

The relative absence of informal-sector activities in the Pacific is partly due to restrictive legislation. There is a "common and pervasive bias against small-scale industrial ventures that are carried out within the purview of the so-called informal sector" (Fairbairn, 1992, p. 24; Connell and Lea, 2002). Only in the market sector of the economy has the informal sector been of considerable local importance, though, in Tonga, success brought about conflict with the formal sector (Brown and Connell, 1993). Throughout the region, there has been little attempt to provide protection and space for the informal sector despite its positive impact on incomes and employment (Connell and Lea, 2002). Urban informal-sector activities are thus usually much less visible than markets and transport, and trivial compared with that of Asian cities.

Small-scale manufacturing activities include domestic work, cooking, tailoring, carpentry and handicraft production, and many tiny businesses operate from homes, producing and selling individual cigarettes, operating *kava* and *sakau* (traditional drinks made from pepper root), and "grog" shops and bars or, beyond the law, engaging in prostitution or marijuana sales (UNDP, 1997, p. 28; Bryant, 1993, p. 78). Many such businesses may be small and short lived, but they generate considerable employment, mainly of youths and often of women. A few have grown, partly by engaging in black-market operations, by incorporating pool (billiards) tables or through particular entrepreneurial skills in good locations. Despite a high level of unemployment, less than 10 per cent of income earners in Blacksands were engaged in informal-sector activities, mainly because the market was small and competition was considerable, and lack of land, skills or licenses prevented success. Work is invariably intermittent, seasonal and poorly rewarded. As in the market sector, women predominate for several reasons: gender discrimination in the formal sector, limited education and skills and the ability to combine informal income-generating activities with a domestic role. Working lives are generally short, hedged in by insecurity, poor conditions and low wages (hence workers simply drift out of work, often as a result of injury or illness, or leave in frustration), made more difficult by limited skills and little job creation. Employment aspirations are far from being satisfied (Mecartney, 2001). Broadly similar conditions occur throughout the subregion, but are much less evident and undocumented in the smaller States. In Samoa, a United Nations agency has recommended that development assistance be targeted towards economically disadvantaged or vulnerable households, some of which were thought to be composed of urban migrants, but it wryly concluded: "there is no data base by which to identify disadvantaged or vulnerable households" (UNDP, 1993, p. 10). The same could be said of most other developing countries and territories in the Pacific.

If markets and small businesses are the positive manifestation of the informal sector, through their contribution to incomes, employment and nutrition, the converse is crime and prostitution, both increasing components of urban employment and lifestyles. The world's oldest trade is now "booming in many Pacific island cities and towns. It is a flourishing industry which evades income tax, brings in foreign exchange, but may prove to be socially and economically costly" (Tara, 1996, p. 22), especially in the capital cities of Melanesia. In Honiara (Solomon Islands), prostitution increased rapidly in the 1990s, taking in school dropouts, unemployed students and some low-income employed, because of domestic problems or the financial burden of a rapidly increasing cost of living. In Fiji, prostitutes are similarly motivated by economic pressures caused by unemployment, divorce, desertion, the failure of men to pay maintenance for their children and lack of assistance from their extended family (Naibavu and Schutz, 1986; Government of Fiji and UNDP, 1997, p. 66). Its economic impact is also significant: "prostitution is a fully localized industry which gives employment to unskilled female workers for most of whom no other jobs are available. It requires no investment of foreign capital, yet it brings in large amounts of foreign exchange with a minimum of leakage back overseas" (Naibavu and Schutz, 1986, p. 98). Prostitution has grown dramatically in Papua New Guinea, especially in Port Moresby, based around hotels and discotheques. In 1995, approximately 38 per cent of otherwise unemployed women were reported to be working as prostitutes – suggesting that there were well over a thousand in the capital – earning more than most employed women (Levantis, 1997). The almost universal rise of prostitution in the Pacific is symptomatic of the problems of limited economic growth, unemployment, the social costs of urbanization, the decline of traditional social control mechanisms and, not least, potentially high earnings. Prostitution poses obvious health problems, including the rapid rise in cases of the human immunodeficiency virus (HIV) and the acquired immunodeficiency syndrome (AIDS) in Papua New Guinea.

Crime, and the resultant acquisition of goods and wealth, is also an informal-sector activity, above all in Papua New Guinea. In Port Moresby, a 1995 survey revealed that a staggering 69 per cent of males, especially youths, who considered themselves to be unemployed, were actually earning a living through crime (which translates to 19 per cent of the entire male urban workforce), and that the incomes obtained through this activity were above those in the formal sector. Hence, few of the euphemistically titled *raskols* (criminals) were actively seeking formal employment, for which they were largely without appropriate skills. Significantly, "*raskols* are doing what the government is unable to do and are redistributing income to the less fortunate who are unable to find formal employment" but at the cost of "stifling any potential growth in output or employment", thus creating a "spiral of disaster" (Levantis, 1997; 2000). Everywhere the informal sector has grown, but most dramatically and painfully in Melanesia, becoming more visible, more significant for income generation, more organized and regulated, but usually poorly understood and rarely officially supported.

Urban unemployment varies significantly between different groups within towns, sometimes according to the time period of movement to the city. Overt unemployment occurs in all urban areas and its extent is increasing. Early studies of urban unemployment in Papua New Guinea in 1973/74 revealed that those out of work tended to come mainly from a small number of relatively poor areas): "Urban unemployment in Papua New Guinea was mainly a phenomenon of the relatively young, the less educated and the more recent arrivals in town. It seems to have been quantitatively most important amongst people from districts very close to the town, and from more distant districts that are poor in services and income-earning opportunities and yet linked into the country's main communications and transport network" (Garnaut and others, 1977, pp. 45, 49, 56). In the previous decade, and especially in the previous five years, unemployment and permanent migration have increased together. At the time of the 1990 census, the overall urban unemployment rate in Papua New Guinea was recorded at 29 per cent but, because of the significance of the informal sector, this was a substantial overestimate (Levantis, 1997, p. 79). A third of adults in the capital were officially searching for formal-sector employment.

Throughout the subregion, unemployment is particularly high among youth (Bryant, 1993, p. 46). In Nuku'alofa (Tonga), the overall unemployment rate in 1986 was 11 per cent (compared with 8 per cent for Tonga as a whole), but for youth aged between 15 and 19, it was as high as 28 per cent and the female rate in this age group was more than 50 per cent, an indication of the growing presence of youth unemployment, despite substantial emigration. Moreover, inadequate access to employment, land and credit have led to increased levels of unemployment in both the small Vava'u town of Neiafu and in Nuku'alofa (Gailey, 1992) and this, in turn, has stimulated emigration. Youth unemployment is also high in Fiji, especially among those with poor educational qualifications in urban areas. It has contributed to growing urban crime problems and substance abuse.

## Poverty and inequality

To some extent, urban poverty is related to internal migration, since it has long been evident, especially in Melanesia, that much migration into urban areas is from impoverished rural areas. That means people are moving away from rural poverty, in the sense of both access to wage- and income-earning opportunities, and access to services (such as health and education). Such migrants are poorly equipped to obtain scarce employment in urban areas and, where they have come from densely populated rural areas such as the Shepherd Islands (Vanuatu) and Simbu (Papua New Guinea), they may be trapped and effectively dispossessed in town. However, nowhere in the Pacific is there information on the extent to which the level of unemployment, or underemployment, is actually greater for relatively recent migrants. In Port Moresby at least this may not be so.

Until quite recently, there was a widespread belief that poverty does not exist in the Pacific, and that if people had difficulties in town they could always return to rural areas. There is now a reluctant recognition that poverty exists, not so much in a monetary sense as in terms of vulnerabilities. One definition of poverty in the Pacific is those "groups of people who do not have access or the means to acquire knowledge, basic services and facilities which is their right" (UNDP, 1996, p. 99). In the case of Vanuatu, the most disadvantaged areas are those distant from the capital with low education, health and income levels, and settlements within the capital. Similar conclusions have been reached in Fiji, where the proportion in poverty is increasing, and in Papua New Guinea (O'Collins, 1999). Isolation emphasizes vulnerability, migration from such remote places has often ensued but has often resulted in urban pockets of poverty rather than new structures of development.

Absolute poverty is not generally apparent in the Pacific subregion; however, some households are poor in the sense that they do not have enough food, clean water or access to an adequate house or basic education (Bryant, 1993, p. 13), but just who comprises these households and where they are is little known. Certainly, poverty is more visible in urban areas, and is most apparent in the larger towns, particularly Port Moresby, where urban social networks have most obviously broken down. Growing unemployment, the rise of the informal sector, including begging and crime, and a range of anecdotal evidence, suggest that urban poverty is increasing.

There is considerable evidence, particularly from the best and most recently documented account – that of Blacksands settlement in Port Vila – that migration transfers rural poverty to urban areas. Inadequate access to incomes and services is more frequent and more problematic in the rural areas of most States, but it is much less visible and spatially concentrated.

In Fiji in the 1990s, around one in every four households was living in poverty, assessed in terms of income levels, housing status and the ability to purchase an adequate diet, and that proportion was almost exactly the same in the urban areas. While the Fiji economy grew by approximately 25 per cent between 1977 and 1991, the proportion of the Fiji population living in poverty actually grew by around two thirds: minimal "trickle down" had occurred, even in a period of relative prosperity, and poverty was actually worsening. Disparities were most evident in the urban areas, and more obvious than they had been a decade previously.

While the greatest extremes of poverty are in settlements, not all those in settlements are poor. In Blacksands, a study found that most households had incomes below the national average, and at least a quarter had problems meeting school fees, paying rents and providing food; some were indebted to kin or friends and some children missed school. Almost half the households supplemented cash incomes with subsistence food gardens. A significant amount of food comes from such gardens, invaluable where urban poverty is worsening and nutrition deteriorating (Soulsby and Murray, 2000). More would have gardens if access to land were possible.

In Suva, the capital of Fiji, where one out of eight people lived in settlements by the mid-1980s, about 12 per cent of these households were living in "cash poverty" (with incomes of less than F\$ 63.10 (around US\$ 40) per week at the end of the decade, and up to 44 per cent were in this status two years later (Bryant, 1992; 1993). The majority of unskilled migrants moving to urban areas have joined increasing numbers of people living in poverty (Prasad and Asafu-Adjaye, 1998). Households with the most diverse income sources (including remittances) fared better than those with only one source. Larger households have tended to fare better, as customary extended household structures have come under increased pressure, and rural "subsistence safety-nets" have collapsed. In Port Vila, as in Suva and Port Moresby, the "urban safety net" of extended kinship (Monsell-Davis, 1993) was declining in significance, as demands on relatives increased. As one woman in Blacksands observed: "The family on the island and the extended family here in Vila always think they can just come and stay whenever they want. The extended family needs to understand that straight family comes first in town" (quoted in Mecartney, 2001, p. 137). Indeed many urban families supported the idea of sending long-term unemployed youth back to the villages.

While many urban households have some access to subsistence incomes, and do benefit from kin support, long-term disadvantaged households that have lost their ability to reciprocate favours may be disowned and ignored even by close relatives. As incomes are increasingly important for food, clothes or school fees, poverty has become of greater socio-economic significance in the absence of adequate or even minimal welfare services. While migrants come to participate in the cash economy, the terms of that participation are so uneven that some people end up struggling to pay for a rented room, and a basic meal of rice and tinned meat or fish: "*Mifala wok long kaikai nomo*" (We're just working for food) (Mitchell, 2000, p. 192). Low incomes and lack of support during illness or unemployment gave a sense of biding time, waiting for unforeseen and uncertain opportunities, and sometimes securing multiple jobs, maintaining strict budgets and abandoning some "traditional" obligations, simply to get by. Many residents survive rather than prosper in the city.

Income inequality is often considerable in urban areas, but its significance is difficult to assess where many households have some access to subsistence resources. However, over time, urban households have become more dependent on the cash economy (partly because of the declining availability of urban land and growing pressure on coastal marine resources). In Vanuatu, for example, a high proportion of the incomes of the urban poor consequently goes into food and rent, and a disproportionate share of the tax burden falls on low-income households, since they spend a higher proportion of their income on highly taxed imported food (Bryant, 1993, p. 38); a similar situation exists in Majuro (Marshall Islands), where access to fresh food is expensive and difficult. In the 1970s, some three quarters of all food consumed in Port Moresby was imported (Flores and Harris, 1982, p. 147) and comparable proportions exist in other towns.

While formal evidence of urban income inequality and other measures of anomie (a situation in which the rules on how people ought to behave with each other are in the process of breaking down and thus people do not know what to expect from one another), such as poverty, malnutrition and social distress, are rare; in many towns, there is a range of visual and anecdotal evidence of difficult urban circumstances, summed up in the case of Fiji. More Fijians are squatting and homeless and landless in towns than ever before. More are found in homes for the destitute, the aged and for abandoned children, and living on an allowance for the destitute.

## CONCLUSION: A SUSTAINABLE FUTURE?

The narrow yet open economies of the Pacific subregion are increasingly influenced by transitions in the international economic system, and particularly the superior growth of countries in the so-called Pacific rim. Foreign investment, tourism, new communications and intensified trade have drawn the Pacific islands more comprehensively into the global system. Increasingly, free trade has seen the gradual dismantling of preferential trade agreements. The challenge to the subregion's economies remains the need to create employment for rising populations with higher expectations, cope with international fluctuations in demand, trade and economic growth, restructure and diversify domestic economies, and gain greater international competitiveness. Declining aid levels emphasize the need for restructuring and privatization (but in circumstances where private sector profitability is limited), though this reduces public sector employment. In the mid-1990s, several States were facing economic and political crises. In particular cases, this situation led to increased emigration; in others, it resulted in acquiescence to Australia's "Pacific solution" of deterring refugees and asylum seekers.

As rural development generates less economic growth and aspirations shift, urbanization has become more evident within the Pacific (and, through emigration, in metropolitan Pacific-rim States). Aspirations to international migration have increased. The island States have sought greater economic diversity through the growth of manufacturing sectors, but without success. Industrial growth is likely to be even slower in the future, despite the liberal terms offered to overseas investors, with the decline of concessional trading schemes. Diversification will be more difficult. Tourism offers prospects for development, but inadequate transport links and intervening opportunities have restricted possibilities.

Uneven development is unlikely to decrease, but while poverty is evident in several States, few Governments recognize its existence, and fewer have sought policy solutions. The interlocking nature of poverty and governance is clear (O'Collins, 1999; Connell and Lea, 2002). Management failure has posed substantial problems of deprivation and inadequate nutrition, and influenced increasing urban crime rates – a far cry from the time when a book on Fiji, Samoa and Tonga could be entitled *Where the Poor are Happy* (Owen, 1955).

The rhetoric of self-reliance, at national and household levels, has disguised a situation in which there has been a growing dependence on external sources of funding, whether from aid, remittances or investment. This has, in part, contributed to new forms of socio-economic inequality in cities, and incipient class formation, though ethnic and regional divisions and traditional power structures are of pervasive importance. International migration has deferred and mitigated, but not resolved, issues of poverty and development. Informal employment is growing faster, as it must, than formal employment, resulting in more complex urban economies, and more complex urban planning and management issues for public services, which are no longer growing. The combination of weak economies, overburdened bureaucracies, urban unemployment, fractured social networks and uneven development challenges the notions of sustainable development.

# REFERENCES

Ahlburg, D. (1991). *Remittances and Their Impact: A Study of Tonga and Western Samoa*, Pacific Policy Papers No. 7, (Canberra, National Centre for Development Studies, Australian National University).

Ahlburg, D. and M. Levin (1990). *The North East Passage: A Study of Pacific Islander Migration to American Samoa and the United States*, (Canberra, National Centre for Development Studies, Australian National University).

Berttram, G. (1999). "The MIRAB model twelve years on", *The Contemporary Pacific*, No. 11, pp. 105-138.

Bertram, G. and R.F. Watters (1985). "The MIRAB economy in South Pacific microstates", *Pacific Viewpoint,* No. 26, pp. 497-520.

Brown, R.P.C. and J. Connell (1993). "The global flea market: Migration, remittances and the informal economy in Tonga", *Development and Change,* No. 24, pp. 611-647.

Bryant, J. (1992). "Poverty in Fiji: Who are the urban poor?", *Singapore Journal of Tropical Geography*, No.13, pp. 90-102.

Bryant, J. (1993). *Urban Poverty and the Environment in the South Pacific*, (Armidale, University of New England).

Chambers, A. (1986). *Reproduction in Nanumea: An Ethnography of Fertility and Birth*, Working Papers in Anthropology No. 72, (Auckland, University of Auckland).

Cobb-Clark, D. and M. Connolly (1997). "A worldwide market for skilled migrants: Can Australia compete?", *International Migration Review*, No. 31, pp. 670-693.

Connell, J. (1988). *Sovereignty and Survival: Island Microstates in the Third World,* Research Monograph No.3, (Sydney, University of Sydney, Department of Geography).

Connell, J. (1997). *Papua New Guinea: The Struggle for Development*, (London, Routledge).

Connell, J. (1999). "Environmental change, economic development and emigration in Tuvalu", *Pacific Studies*, No. 22, pp. 1-20.

Connell, J. (2001). *The Migration of Skilled Health Personnel in the Pacific Region*, (Sydney, University of Sydney for the World Health Organization).

Connell, J and R. Brown (1995). "Migration and remittances in the South Pacific: Towards new perspectives", *Asian and Pacific Migration Journal*, No. 4, pp. 1-34.

Connell, J. and J. Lea (2002). *Urbanisation in the Island Pacific*, (London, Routledge).

Cook Islands (1984). *Cook Islands Development Plan*, (Rarotonga, Cook Islands).

Cowling, W. (1990). "Motivations for contemporary Tongan migration", in, P.Herda, J. Terrell and N. Gunson (eds.), *Tongan Culture and History*, (Canberra, Australian National University).

Dyson, T. (1982). *The South Seas Dream*, (London, Heinemann).

Fairbairn, T. (1992). *The Role of Small-Scale Industry in Pacific Island Countries*, University of New South Wales Pacific Studies Monograph No. 4, (Sydney, UNSW).

Flores, A. and G. Harris (1982). "The marketing of fresh fruit and vegetables in Port Moresby", *Pacific Viewpoint*, No. 23, pp. 147-160.

Gailey, C. W. (1992). "State formation, development and social change in Tonga", in, A. Robillard (ed.), *Social Change in the Pacific Islands,* (London, Kegan Paul International).

Garnaut, R., M. Wright and R. Curtain (1977). *Employment Incomes and Migration in Papua New Guinea Towns*, Institute of Applied Social and Economic Research Monograph No. 6, (Port Moresby, IASER).

Goddard, M. (1992). "Big man thief: The social organisation of gangs in Port Moresby", *Canberra Anthropology*, No. 15, pp. 20-34.

Goddard, M. (2001). "From rolling thunder to reggae: Imagining squatter settlements in Papua New Guinea", *The Contemporary Pacific*, No. 13, pp. 1-32.

Government of Fiji and UNDP (1997). *Fiji Poverty Report*, (Suva, UNDP).

Hardaker, J. and others *(1987)*. *Smallholder Agriculture in Tonga,* (Armidale, University of New England).

Hezel, F. and M. Levin (1996). "New trends in Micronesian migration: FSM migration to Guam and the Marinas, 1990-1993", *Pacific Studies*, No.19, pp. 91-114.

Hooker, K. and J. Varcoe (1999). "Migration and the Cook Islands", in, J. Overton and R. Scheyvens (eds.), *Strategies for Sustainable Development Experiences from the Pacific*, (Sydney, University of New South Wales Press), pp. 91-99.

Iredale, Robyn (2000). "Skilled migration policies in the Asia-Pacific region", *International Migration Review*, vol. 34, pp. 882-906.

International Organization for Migration (IOM) and United Nations (2000). *World Migration Report: 2000,* (Geneva, IOM and United Nations).

Jackson, R.T. (1976). *An Introduction to the Urban Geography of Papua New Guinea*, (Port Moresby, University of Papua New Guinea).

Johannes, R. (1981). *Words of the Lagoon: Fishing and Marine Lore in the Palau District of Micronesia*, (Berkeley, University of California Press).

Karakita, Y. (1997). Prior to MIRAB?: "Remittances and inter-island relations in Woleai Atoll, Yap State, Federated States of Micronesia", in, K.Sudo and S. Yoshida (eds.), *Contemporary Migration in Oceania: Diaspora and Network*, (Osaka, Japan Center for Area Studies), pp. 11-24.

Koczberski, G., G. Curry and J. Connell (2001). "Full circle or spiralling out of control? State violence and the control of urbanisation in Papua New Guinea", *Urban Studies*, No. 38, pp. 2017-2026.

Levantis, T. (1997). "Urban unemployment in Papua New Guinea: It's criminal", *Pacific Economic Bulletin*, vol. 12, No. 2, pp. 73-84.

Liki, A. (1994). E Tele A'a o le Tagata: Career Choices of Samoan Professionals within and beyond their Nu'u Moni, (unpublished M.A. thesis, University of the South Pacific, Suva).

McMurray, C. (1992). "Issues in population planning: The case of Papua New Guinea", *Development Bulletin*, No. 24, pp. 13-16.

Macpherson, C. (1992). "Economic and political restructuring and the sustainability of migrant remittances: The case of Western Samoa", *The Contemporary Pacific*, No. 4, pp. 109-136.

Macpherson, C. and L. Macpherson, (1987). "Toward an explanation of recent trends in suicide in Western Samoa", *Man*, No. 22, pp. 305-330.

Marcus, G.E. (1981). "Power on the extreme periphery: The perspective of Tongan elites in the modern world system", *Pacific Viewpoint*, No. 22, pp. 48-64.

Marcus, G.E. (1993). "Tonga's contemporary globalizing strategies: Trading on sovereignty amidst international migration", in, T. Harding and B. Wallace (eds.), *Contemporary Pacific Societies*, (Englewood Cliffs, New Jersey, Prentice Hall), pp. 21-33.

Maron, N. (2001). *Return to Nukunuku: Identity, Culture and Return Migration in Tonga*, (Sydney, School of Geosciences).

Mecartney, S. (2001). Blacksands Settlement: Towards Urban Permanence in Vanuatu, (unpublished M.A. thesis, University of Sydney).

Mitchell, J. (2000). "Violence as continuity: Violence as rupture: Narratives from an urban settlement in Vanuatu", in, S. Dinnen and A. Ley (eds.), *Reflections on Violence in Melanesia*, (Sydney, Hawkins Press), pp. 189-208.

Monsell-Davis, M. (1993). "Urban exchange: Safety net or disincentive? Wantoks or relatives in the urban Pacific", *Canberra Anthropology*, No. 16, pp. 45-66.

Munro, D. (1990). "Transnational corporations of kin and the MIRAB system: The case of Tuvalu", *Pacific Viewpoint*, No. 31, pp. 63-66.

Munro, D. and R. Bedford (1980). "Historical backgrounds", in *A Report on the Results of the Census of Tuvalu*, (Funafuti, Government of Tuvalu), pp. 1-13.

Naibavu, T. and B. Schutz (1986). "Prostitution: Problem or profitable industry?", in, C. Griffin and M. Monsell Davis (eds.), *Fijians in Town*, (Suva, Institute of Pacific Studies), pp. 89-101.

Nibbrig, N. (1992). "Rascals in paradise: Urban gangs in Papua New Guinea", *Pacific Studies*, No. 15, pp. 115-134.

O'Collins, M. (1999). "Reflections on poverty assessments in Papua New Guinea, Fiji and Vanuatu", *Pacific Economic Bulletin*, vol. 14, No.1, pp. 33-46.

Ogden, M. (1994). "MIRAB and the Republic of the Marshall Islands", *Isla*, No. 2, pp. 237-272.

Owen, R. (1955). *Where the Poor are Happy*, (London, Collins).

Prasad, B. and J. Asafu-Adjaye (1998). "Macroconomic policy and poverty in Fiji", *Pacific Economic Bulletin*, vol. 13, No. 1, pp. 47-56.

Rehuher, F. (1993). "Comments on youth development and movement: Providing an alternative to urban drift, a Palau case", in *The Family in the Aquatic Continent*, (Maui, Hawaii, Maui Pacific Center), pp. 21-24.

Shankman, P. (1993). "The Samoan exodus", in, V. Lockwood and others (eds.), *Contemporary Pacific Societies*, (Englewood Cliffs, New Jersey, Prentice Hall), pp. 156-170.

Shore, B. (1978). "Introduction", in, C. Macpherson and others (eds.), *New Neighbors: Islanders in Adaptation*, (Santa Cruz, Center for South Pacific Studies, University of California), pp. xiii-xiv.

Soulsby, J. and W. Murray (2000). Urban agriculture: Food security and new urban poor, (Suva, unpublished mimeo).

Small, C. (1997). *Voyages: From Tongan Villages to American Suburbs*, (Ithaca, New York, Cornell University Press).

Smith, D. (1996). "Palauans in Guam", *Micronesian Counselor*, August, pp. 6-20.

Tara, T. (1996). "Prostitution: A growing problem in Honiara", *Islands Business*, vol. 22, No. 8, pp. 22-23.

Tongamoa, T. (1987). Migration, Remittances and Development: A Tongan Perspective, (unpublished M.A. thesis, University of Sydney).

United Nations Development Programme (UNDP) (1993). *Report of Joint UNDP/ SPC Mission to Western Samoa*, (Suva, UNDP).

United Nations Development Programme (UNDP) (1996). *Sustainable Human Development in Vanuatu*, (Suva, UNDP).

United Nations Development Programme (UNDP) (1997). *Sustaining Livelihoods: Promoting Informal Sector Growth in Pacific Island Countries*, (Suva, UNDP).

Vavine, P. (1984). "Ivane settlement: A case study of first generation migrants to Port Moresby", *Ambio*, No. 13, p. 309.

Walsh, A.C. (1982). *Migration, Urbanization and Development in South Pacific Countries*, Country Report No. 6, (New York, United Nations).

# CHAPTER III

# COMPARATIVE MIGRATION POLICIES
# IN THE ESCAP REGION

By Patcharawalai Wongboonsin[*]

International migration, as an intrinsic part of the development process, can be traced far back into the history of the ESCAP region and each individual country and area comprising it. The changing differentials in income and employment opportunities as well as the inequalities in demographic and social development among countries in the region during the past few decades have led to changing patterns in the magnitude, structure and complexity of international migration. One of the most salient problems of the ESCAP region today is the cross-border migration of both documented and undocumented migrants. Such movement of people is often seen as a threat to national security and a cause of many social problems in the countries of destination. At the same time, certain countries have seen the concrete contribution that international migration has made in their national economic development process. Migration policies have, therefore, become an important policy issue for the Governments of many countries in the region. In a study of the evolution of the perceptions and policies on international migration, the United Nations (1998a; 1998b) noted changes in Governments' perceptions of migration trends during the second half of the 1970s and early 1980s. As the pattern, magnitude and structure of international migration keeps on changing in complex ways, this paper examines current migration policies to identify disparities and common features in the ESCAP region. It focuses on international migration, both documented and undocumented, and considers the perspectives of both sending and receiving countries. National policies on forced migration are also included.

[*]Assistant Director and Senior Researcher/Expert, Institute of Asian Studies, Chulalongkorn University, Bangkok.

# SENDING COUNTRIES

## South-East Asia

All South-East Asian countries, irrespective of economic development levels and population size, have a number of their human resources overseas. However, not all of the countries have adopted policies to export their workforce (table 1). This is particularly the case for Brunei Darussalam, Cambodia, the Lao People's Democratic Republic and Malaysia. Most South-East Asian countries with a workforce export policy expect contributions of emigration to the national economy through remittances. After the financial crisis of 1997/98, most Governments of countries in South-East Asia with a workforce export policy not only stepped up exports, but have also reconsidered their regulatory regimes to reach their export goals. Among these countries, the degree of governmental intervention has varied.

A strong interventionist approach of a workforce export policy is seen in the case of Myanmar and Viet Nam. Since the 1980s, the Vietnamese Government has considered migration for overseas employment to be an important element of its employment policies. Workforce export is also used as a policy measure to regulate social and regional imbalances in Viet Nam. That Government has adopted a policy of centrally controlled and planned workforce export based on bilateral cooperation agreements with receiving countries. This began with the export of its workforce to Czechoslovakia and the former Union of Soviet Socialist Republics (USSR) in the early 1980s, followed by Algeria and Iraq in the mid-1980s, Bulgaria and Germany in the late 1980s and Kuwait in the 1990s. The initial plan to export skilled workers is currently shifting towards unskilled workers. Lately, the Government has considered Japan and the Republic of Korea as the target destinations for unskilled workers under on-the-job training programmes (Dang, 1998). According to a recent government policy to step up exports, about 50,000 workers were expected to have taken overseas employment in 2001. This compares with 31,400 workers sent abroad in 1999 (*Migration News*, February 2001). A unique feature of Viet Nam's emigration policy compared with that of other South-East Asian countries is that Viet Nam has relied on State-owned corporations to organize emigration. This strategy is similar to that of China.

As in Viet Nam, the Myanmar Department of Labour has been collabourating with countries of destination in finding overseas employment. As an additional

## Table 1. Migration policies in sending countries: South-East Asia

| Country | Labour export policy | | |
|---|---|---|---|
| | No labour export policy | Non-interventionist policy of labour export | Interventionist policy of labour export |
| Brunei Darussalam | No labour export policy | - | - |
| Cambodia | No labour export policy | - | - |
| Indonesia | - | - | Before 1994, policy to promote unskilled, uneducated emigration; currently maintains policy to prioritize skilled and educated emigration and to minimize unskilled, uneducated emigration; not much effort in terms of training programmes. |
| Lao People's Democratic Republic | No labour export policy | - | - |
| Malaysia | No labour export policy | - | - |
| Myanmar | - | - | A strongly interventionist policy of labour export based on bilateral labour-service agreement with receiving countries. |
| Philippines | - | - | To promote overseas employment at all levels of skills with an active policy to protect migrants; recent initiatives: to deregulate recruitment agencies; to encourage the international community to allow free movement of labour at all skill levels. |
| Singapore | - | Encouraging overseas employment with a non-interventionist policy | - |
| Thailand | - | - | Recent more active policy to promote trained migrant workers with more active role of the State in terms of labour training and marketing; a bilateral labour service agreement with receiving countries serves as an extra measure. |
| Viet Nam | - | - | A strongly interventionist policy of centrally controlled and planned labour export based on bilateral labour service agreements with receiving countries. |

measure to those adopted in other sending countries in South-East Asia, the Myanmar Government has played a role in providing economic migrants with information on policies and regulations governing the admission and stay of migrants in certain countries of destination. The Government has encouraged the return of its economic migrants on a voluntary basis (Myint, 1998). However, to assure the contribution of emigration to the national economy, the Government requires its overseas workers to pay a 10 per cent tax on their earnings. According to *Migration News* (June 2000), beginning in March 2000, migrants from Myanmar are also required to give half their earnings to local Myanmar embassies as funds for their relatives.

The Philippines is another country that encourages overseas employment at all levels of skill. Compared with other South-East Asian countries, the Philippines has adopted a relatively active policy to protect its workforce abroad. The enactment of the Migrant Workers and Overseas Filipino Act of 1995 serves to protect the interests and promote the welfare of over 6 million Filipinos working in approximately 140 countries around the world.

Immediately after the 1997/98 financial crisis, the Government of the Philippines expanded the scope of the emigration regulatory regimes and strengthened the mandate of existing mechanisms that monitor and manage the overseas employment programme. The year 2000 was proclaimed as the year of Overseas Filipino Migrants. A policy shift took place when the Philippines aimed at further boosting exports in the current era of competitive world markets. This is seen in a policy to deregulate recruitment agencies (*Migration News*, May 2001). Complementary measures include calls for the free movement of people at all levels of skill, the liberalization of government controls, and the strengthening of State protection of migrant workers.

Compared with other South-East Asian countries, the Philippines has recently been active in addressing the problem of human trafficking. A strategy of the Philippines Government is to rely on regional forums such as the Asian Regional Initiative against the Trafficking of Women and Children. The Global Program against Trafficking in Human Beings was also established in 2000 in the Philippines with the participation of various government agencies and in cooperation with the United Nations Centre for International Crime Prevention (Scalabrini Migration Center, 2000).

In contrast to the Philippines, Indonesia has adopted a selective approach in terms of workforce export. A policy to encourage high numbers of unskilled, uneducated workers to work abroad characterized Indonesia prior to the start of its Sixth Five-Year Development Plan (1994-1998). The Indonesian Government has recently shifted its policy towards the reduction of uneducated/unskilled worker emigration and the prioritization of sending skilled and educated workers abroad in order to meet the challenges of the competitive world market and to gain more remittances. Under the new policy, the export of untrained workers is subject to a quota system. However, the policy has been criticized as aggravating the problem of undocumented migration from Indonesia. According to Tjiptoherijanto (1998, p. 6), the Indonesian Government has spared little effort in strengthening its human resources; it has emphasized the adjustment and upgrading of its policies and regulations so that educated and skilled workers would be encouraged to work abroad.

On the other hand, the Thai Government recently initiated an effort to upgrade its workforce through training programmes before emigration. It is part of a new Thai policy since the 1997/98 financial crisis to actively promote emigration to competitive markets worldwide. In 1998, Thailand set a goal to send 210,000 workers abroad in the hope of easing unemployment at home and of earning more than 100,000 million baht (US$ 1 = around 38 baht in 1998) in remittances. The Thai Government has also strengthened its efforts in marketing and overseas employment protection. An action plan on overseas employment is being drafted.

Singapore is no exception in encouraging its nationals to work overseas, with the expectation that the migrants will use their experience to contribute to the economy upon returning to their homeland. According to emigration regulatory regimes in that country, Singaporeans are virtually free to move out of the country; there is no legal barrier to prevent Singaporeans from emigrating. The only exception is for male citizens at the age of national military service. What the Singaporean Government is doing to avoid the potential brain drain is to help their expatriates remain rooted (Yap, 1998).

### East Asia

As in Viet Nam and Myanmar in South-East Asia, China has relied upon bilateral service agreements or direct employment with countries of destination. According to its Ministry of Foreign Trade and Economic Cooperation, by 1994 China had developed such a cooperation programme with more than 50 countries around the world (Tseng, 2001). Recently, China has adopted unique policy measures to manage orderly emigration flows in response to concerns raised in a number of destination countries that China is a source of undocumented

71

## Table 2. Migration policies in sending countries: East Asia, South Asia and Pacific islands

| Country or area | Labour export policy | | |
|---|---|---|---|
| | No labour export policy | Non-interventionist policy of labour export | Interventionist policy of labour export |
| Bangladesh | - | - | An active policy to promote emigration of labour at all skill levels with institutional mechanisms to monitor and control the performance of recruitment agencies, welfare attachés and welfare funds. |
| China (mainland) | - | - | Policy to regulate and manage orderly emigration with bilateral agreements on labour service or direct employment; to decide a daily quota on labour emigration to Hong Kong, China. |
| Hong Kong, China | - | A non-interventionist policy | - |
| India | No policy to encourage labour emigration but to regulate emigration and to protect migrant workers. Recently began minimizing certain restrictions so as not to lose out in the international market. | - | - |
| Pacific islands | - | Not a policy issue. | - |
| Pakistan | - | - | A policy to promote emigration with minimal controls; relying on close political and economic ties with major destination countries; institutional mechanisms to monitor and control the performance of recruitment agencies, welfare attachés and welfare funds. |
| Sri Lanka | - | - | An active policy to promote emigration of labour at all skill levels with institutional mechanisms to monitor and control the performance of recruitment agencies, welfare attachés and welfare funds. |

migration. As part of its tough measures, China has recently cracked down not only on illegal emigration but also on people-smugglers. Under the new law, the latter are subject to imprisonment for one year. China has also signed a bilateral agreement with Hong Kong, China to establish a daily quota system on emigration to that Special Administrative Region. Despite these efforts, it is not easy to root out the causes of illegal migration in the short term owing to a number of complex factors (*Migration News*, March 2001).

Hong Kong, China's policy towards emigration of workers is closer to that of Singapore than that of China. It has adopted a laissez-faire policy of non-intervention towards emigration. According to the Basic Law, residents of Hong Kong, China have the right to move freely within the Hong Kong, China Special Administrative Region, and have the freedom of emigration to other countries and regions (AMPRN, 1998) (see table 2).

## South Asia

In contrast to South-East Asian countries, India has no policy to encourage the emigration of its workforce. This is due to the fact that remittances are not seen in India as a driving force for emigration. However, in order not to lose out in the market, India has minimized certain restrictions while maintaining the policy of protecting and regulating the flow of its workforce. The Emigration Act was first enacted in 1922 as the main legislative mechanism to implement the policy. Under the Act, an unskilled or semi-skilled worker is required to obtain "emigration clearance" from the Protector General of Emigrants before leaving the country. This institutional mechanism has offices in different States. The Emigration Act of 1983 was designed to be a more comprehensive piece of legislation than the 1922 version of the law. It governs the emigration of Indian workers for overseas employment on a contractual basis. It also safeguards the interests and ensures the welfare of overseas Indian workers (Premi and Mathur, 1995; Shah, 1995, p. 582). While the Philippines is deregulating recruitment agencies, India maintains that only properly registered recruiting agents can conduct the business of recruitment for overseas employment. The Protector of Emigration is entitled to take into account recruiting agents' financial soundness, trustworthiness, experience etc.

Bangladesh and Sri Lanka have actively promoted the emigration of workers at all skill levels. In Sri Lanka, this policy has been supported by the following measures: devaluation of the national currency; relaxation of exchange controls; ability of overseas workers to open foreign currency accounts; minimization of restrictions on travel and the issuance of passports. The Foreign Employment

Assistance Centre has also been established to assist migrants with the issuance of passports, banking and registration documents etc. As in India, the Bureau of Manpower, Employment and Training and the Bureau of Foreign Employment have been established in Bangladesh and Sri Lanka, respectively in order to manage orderly emigration. These institutional mechanisms have been established to monitor and control the performance of recruitment agents and to determine the fees migrant workers are charged. As in India, Bangladesh and Sir Lanka have also relied upon welfare attachés appointed to embassies and a welfare fund to which the workers contribute upon departure. The welfare fund is designed to serve two purposes: to make payments to the family of a worker who dies overseas and to ensure that the workers emigrate only through licensed recruitment agents. Recently, the Government of Sri Lanka has adopted a policy to diversify the workforce export market to unfamiliar destinations. Policy measures include, for example, market promotion campaigns, employment promotion tours, training programmes and cooperation with licensed recruitment agencies. At the same time, the Government has kept an eye on factors such as a possible negative impact from a shortage of workers at home (Shah, 1995, p. 594).

As in the case of Bangladesh and Sri Lanka, Pakistan's migration policy is aimed at maximizing emigration. It has also minimized controls on workforce emigration. However, the Government has been criticized for having done less than its neighbours to achieve its objectives. Rather, it has relied on close political and economic ties with major destination countries, according to Shah (1995, p. 582).

The Russian Federation, as in Hong Kong, China and Singapore, has adopted a laissez-faire policy towards emigration. The new Russian constitution since 1993 guarantees freedom of movement as one of the basic rights of Russian citizens to emigrate temporarily or permanently in search of better opportunities (Codagnone, 1998).

## Pacific island countries and territories

In contrast to other subregions, policies to address the issue of transnational migration in the less developed countries and territories of the Pacific are implicit rather than explicit. According to the United Nations (1996, p. 219), a major reason is domestic disagreement about the impact of emigration, that is, whether it contributes to economic growth or delays the prospects for economic development. Moreover, transnational migration is negligible in Melanesia. An exception is Fiji, where the emigration of skilled and professional workers increased in the 1990s owing to political instability. However, emigration is of little concern at the policy level there. At the same time, transnational migration is common between island States in Polynesia and developed countries with which they have historical ties.

# RECEIVING COUNTRIES

## South-East Asia

The major receiving countries in South-East Asia include Malaysia, Singapore and Thailand, none of which are parties to the 1951 Convention Relating to the Status of Refugees and/or Its 1967 Protocol (table 3). Singapore has adopted a three-tiered migration scheme for foreign workers, besides social visits. First, there is an economy-driven migration scheme for professional foreign workers, including those holding administrative positions as well as professional and managerial positions. Singapore has recently strengthened its efforts to encourage such high-end migrant workers to contribute to the economy through a liberalized policy with special treatments for their entry, employment and stay. They are encouraged to settle down and integrate into Singapore society.

Second, there is a scheme for workers of relatively lower calibre, including skilled workers and technicians. They are allowed to work in all sectors of the economy, to bring in their dependants and to marry Singaporeans.

Third, there is a scheme for unskilled and semi-skilled contract foreigners to work only in approved sectors. These workers are to be repatriated once their contracts expire. The employment of migrant workers in the third scheme is subject to dependency ceilings in each industry and a levy on firms employing foreign workers. The Singaporean regulatory regimes governing the employment of the migrant workers in this third scheme aim at ensuring that firms employ foreign workers only because they cannot find suitably qualified locals rather than because of their desire for cheap labour. In addition, they can marry Singaporeans only with the approval of the Government and are not permitted to bring in their dependants. Female unskilled and semi-skilled contract migrant workers are deported if they are found to be pregnant. The migrant workers in this third scheme are further differentiated into three types according to the countries or areas of origin: (a) those from traditional sources: Malaysia; (b) those from North and East Asian sources: Hong Kong, China; Macao, China; the Republic of Korea; and Taiwan Province of China; and (c) those from non-traditional sources: Bangladesh, India, Indonesia, Myanmar, the Philippines, Sri Lanka and Thailand.

## Table 3. Migration policies of receiving countries: South-East Asia

| Country | Policy towards forced migration | Policy towards job-oriented migration | |
|---|---|---|---|
| | Signatory to the 1951 Convention and Its 1967 Protocol | Documented migrants | Undocumented migrants |
| Indonesia | No | Urging transfers of technology to local workforce. | - |
| Malaysia | No | Unskilled/semi-skilled migrants can be employed in only a few sectors and are limited to nationals of a few countries in South and South-East Asia; recent policy to minimize dependence on unskilled/ semi-skilled migrants. | To toughen border controls with preventive measures and amnesty programmes. |
| Myanmar | No | Only under work contracts with the Government or private enterprises. | Surveillance along the border by Team for Prevention of Illegal Immigrants. |
| Philippines | Yes | Unskilled migrant labour is prohibited; foreign workers can be employed only because firms cannot find suitably qualified locals; urging transfer of technology to local workforce. | A policy to toughen border controls with preventive measures and amnesty programmes. |
| Singapore | No | Recently, a more open policy for high-end migrant workers; a more restrictive policy for low-end migrant labour. | Recent policy to toughen border controls with preventive measures. |
| Thailand | Policy to provide humanitarian relief | Unskilled migrant workers being prohibited from entry and employment; alien employment is allowed in all sectors, except for 39 jobs prohibited by law. | Recent policy to toughen border controls with preventive measures; non-universal amnesty programme (undocumented migrants from Cambodia, the Lao People's Democratic Republic, Myanmar and Viet Nam are allowed to work in certain jobs and areas after registration). |

Different regulations apply to migrant workers from different types of sources. Recently, Singapore has pushed certain industries to train their unskilled and semi-skilled migrant workers through various incentives to learn updated skills so as to achieve higher productivity. The construction industry is a case in point. This represents a unique approach compared with other receiving countries in the region (Wongboonsin, 2000).

Unlike Singapore, the Malaysian Government acknowledges two major categories of foreign workers: *pekerja ikhtisas,* or expatriates or skilled and professional workers; and *pekerja asing* or foreign workers at lower skill levels employed temporarily on a contract basis through recruitment agencies, with lower wages and lower entitlements. Malaysia's policy towards alien workers is more like that of the Philippines than that of Singapore. As in the Philippines, Malaysia's restrictive measures apply to foreign workers at all skill levels. They can be employed only in approved economic sectors. The regulatory regimes in both Malaysia and the Philippines are aimed at ensuring that firms employ foreign workers only because they cannot find suitably qualified locals rather than because of their desire for cheap labour. So far, semi-skilled and unskilled workers are permitted to work only in four sectors in Malaysia: plantation, construction, manufacturing and services. The latter includes positions as household maids, petrol pump attendants, and waiters and waitresses. Moreover, foreign workers permitted to work in the above-mentioned sectors are limited to nationals from Bangladesh, Indonesia, Pakistan, the Philippines and Thailand. For household maids, only nationals of Indonesia, the Philippines and Thailand are permitted entry for employment. Employers in Sabah are permitted to employ workers from Indonesia and the Philippines only. At the same time, employers in the Federal Territory of Labuan are permitted to employ workers from Bangladesh, Indonesia, Pakistan, the Philippines and Thailand only. The employers in both areas are also subject to obtaining a license from the Sabah Department and approval quota for employing foreign workers from the Committee of Indonesian Foreign Workers in Sabah and the Federal Territory of Labuan. Employers in Sarawak are required to obtain a license and recruitment quota from the Sarawak Department (Wongboonsin, 2001a).

In both Malaysia and the Philippines, foreign companies are allowed to bring the required personnel to areas where there is a shortage of trained local workers to do the job. In both countries, expatriate migrants can engage only in key management positions or in jobs requiring specialized skills not available among the local workforce. Besides, employing companies are required to make every effort to train more local workers (Wongboonsin, 2001a).

77

This latter approach is also found in Indonesia. While Indonesian migrant workers are mainly uneducated and unskilled, foreign workers in Indonesia are mainly professional and managerial. Indonesian immigration policy allows the use of foreign manpower selectively in the framework of the optimum efficient use of Indonesian manpower and in order to promote the transfer of technology (Tjiptoherijanto, 1998, p. 4).

Malaysia is following a regional trend towards reducing dependence on foreign workers at lower skill levels, while prioritizing the employment of the local workforce. This recent Malaysian policy is based on the Government's vision of building a "knowledge economy", with greater automation and labour-saving technologies in production processes. During this transitional period, the Malaysian Government has set targets to increase the number of professional foreign workers by 5,000. In February 2000, the Cabinet Committee on Foreign Workers announced a list of 138 skilled and semi-skilled jobs prohibited for foreign workers. This is a measure similar to that adopted earlier in Thailand. Jobs prohibited for foreign workers in Malaysia include, for example, musicians, *haj* (Muslim pilgramage) executives, tour executives, catering executives, mechanical machinery operators, insurance agents, real estate agents, share dealers (*Migration News*, March 2000).

Unlike Malaysia and Singapore, the Thai migration policy and regulatory regimes do not allow the entry and employment of unskilled migrant workers. Its migration policy to prohibit the entry and employment of unskilled migrant workers is similar to that of Japan, the Philippines and the Republic of Korea.

While most receiving countries in the ESCAP region provide a list of occupations or economic sectors allowed for alien recruitment, the Thai regulatory regimes identify 39 jobs or occupations prohibited to aliens for employment in all areas of the country. The list includes unskilled, semi-skilled and skilled jobs, and is based on the fact that these are jobs already being performed by Thai nationals.

The 1997/98 financial crisis has prompted Malaysia, Singapore and Thailand to toughen their border controls and other preventive measures against undocumented migrants. According to the new Singaporean Immigration (Amendment) Bill 1998, attempting illegal entry is subject to a penalty equivalent to illegal entry and departure. Both Singapore and Malaysia have strengthened efforts to combat the activities of syndicates and other unscrupulous persons luring undocumented migrants into Malaysia. Malaysia's Cabinet Committee on Illegal Immigrants recently proposed an amendment to Section 6(3) of the

Immigration Act to increase the current fine of up to 10,000 ringgits (US$ 1 = M$ 3.80) or jail term of up to five years or both for foreigners entering the country illegally. The Committee has also proposed an increase in fines on employers and the introduction of new fines for those harbouring illegal foreigners (*Migration News*, September 2001; Wongboonsin, 2000).

To cope with the problem of undocumented unskilled migrant workers and the structural adjustment to the lack of local workers in certain labour-intensive and unskilled economic activities, Thailand has adopted an amnesty programme, with a tightening of border control measures, as has been done in Malaysia and many other countries around the world. Under the Thai amnesty programme, employers in some industries and some provinces are permitted to legally employ undocumented unskilled migrants after registration. Such migrants are allowed to work in specified jobs unlikely to be performed by local workers. However, the programme applies only to migrants from Cambodia, the Lao People's Democratic Republic, Myanmar and Viet Nam (Wongboonsin, 2000).

Despite being a non-signatory to the aforementioned 1951 Convention and having no refugee migration scheme, Thailand maintains a policy to provide humanitarian relief for forced migration. For example, it has allowed ethnic minorities from Myanmar to stay in designated areas inside Thailand.

Policies dealing with the immigration of foreign workers are a comparatively recent phenomenon in Myanmar. Since the shift in the State Economic Policy towards a market-oriented economy, Myanmar has allowed foreigners to enter the country for employment, business and social matters. However, compared with other countries in the region, international immigration to Myanmar is limited. According to the current State rules and regulations, embassies and consulates abroad have been given the authority to issue "entry visas" to foreigners at their discretion. Foreigners holding such a visa are allowed to stay up to one month in Myanmar. Experts or technicians are allowed to work in Myanmar only under work contracts with the Myanmar Government or with private enterprises. Only tourist visa regulations have been simplified and relaxed. Since March 1994, the validity period of a tourist visa has been extended to 28 days and is normally non-extendable. An exception exists for those granted special permission by the Ministry of Hotels and Tourism. In terms of settlement, Myanmar has adopted a closed immigration policy with enforcement of the *Foreigner's Act* governing permanent foreign settlers. Accordingly, most foreigners enter on a temporary basis rather than to settle in that country.

## Table 4. Migration policies of receiving countries: East Asia

| Country or area | Policy towards forced migration | Policy towards job-oriented migration | |
|---|---|---|---|
| | Signatory to the 1951 Convention and Its 1967 Protocol | Documented migrants | Undocumented migrants |
| Japan | Recent policy to curb influx of refugees | A highly restrictive migration policy based on three fundamental tenets: (a) admitting foreign workers as the last resort; (b) no unskilled labour to be admitted; (c) foreign workers to be employed only on a temporary basis. A trainee system is maintained as a de facto temporary worker scheme to solve the problem of labour shortages at the unskilled level. | To toughen border controls with preventive measures; to crack down on overstayers; amnesty programmes. |
| Hong Kong, China | Yes | A restrictive labour import policy; a strict quota system for expatriates and professional migrants; no quota restriction for foreign domestic workers; a tighter control with daily quota restrictions for migrants from mainland China. | Strict control over undocumented immigration, with immediate deportation. |
| Republic of Korea | No | A highly restrictive migration policy with a move to transform the foreign trainee system into a guest-worker scheme. | A more humanitarian policy towards undocumented migrants. |
| Taiwan Province of China | No | A policy to centrally plan and control the flows of migrant workers at all levels, with careful selection of foreign workers from a limited number of countries which render diplomatic support to Taiwan Province of China; a policy to regularize and legalize the employment of unskilled migrant workers in certain sectors; to issue permanent residence permits to some aliens; to open more jobs to professionals and highly skilled foreign workers. | Strict border and residence controls. |

Recently, Myanmar has opened border check points to allow passage and permit border trade with neighbouring countries, namely, Bangladesh, China, India, the Lao People's Democratic Republic and Thailand. A bilateral agreement with Thailand for legal travel via border check points was concluded in 1997. At the same time, surveillance is maintained along the 6,250 km border to prevent undocumented entry and exit. The Team for the Prevention of Illegal Immigrants has served as a key institutional mechanism to enforce the Myanmar Immigration (Emergency Provision) Act of 1947. In terms of forced migration, Myanmar has a policy to rely on bilateral agreements for repatriation activities (Myint, 1998; Wongboonsin, 2000).

## East Asia

Among East Asian countries, Japan and the Republic of Korea have shared similar features in terms of migration policies towards labour migrants until the beginning of the twenty-first century (table 4). Both countries have recently shifted their positions from being major sending countries to being receiving countries. Owing to the lack of consensus within the Governments on the issue of foreign workers, both Japan and the Republic of Korea can be classified as countries without explicit policies to import workers. While Japan has insisted on maintaining its highly restrictive migration policy, the Republic of Korea is moving towards the establishment of a migration system that would open its market to foreign workers, including the unskilled. This move can be seen from a plan announced by the Government of the Republic of Korea in 2000 to turn trainees into foreign workers entitled to minimum wages and benefits similar to those enjoyed by Korean workers. As in Japan, the trainee system was previously adopted as an instrument, or a de facto temporary worker scheme, to solve the problem of shortages at the level of unskilled workers. In September 2001, the Ministry of Labour proposed a revision of the foreign trainee system under which trainee status is limited to one year, followed by two years of guest-worker status (*Migration News*, 8/9, September 2001). The Republic of Korea is considering the adoption of training programmes for migrant workers in certain sectors to help them to adapt to the local business environment. Initially, this refers to the information technology sector in the Republic of Korea, according to a proposal made by the Ministry of Information and Communications in June 2001. In recognition of the structural demand on the unskilled migrant, one may expect in the near future the adoption of a policy towards immigration in the Republic of Korea that is clearer than the one in Japan. This is so despite the fact that the immigration law of the Republic of Korea restricts the admission of foreign workers to fewer categories than that of Japan.

81

With regard to the problem of undocumented migrant workers, an amnesty programme for persons overstaying their visas was first adopted by the Republic of Korea in June 1992, allowing those reporting to the authorities to stay in the country until December 1992. The deadline was extended from time to time. By the late 1990s, the Government adopted a more humanitarian policy towards undocumented migrant workers, as can be seen from a government-run industrial accident insurance scheme covering undocumented migrant workers on equal terms with local workers (AMPRN, 1997). To cope with smugglers, the Republic of Korea has adopted a policy to strengthen monitoring of the transit area and to work with airlines to identify boarding-pass swappers (*Migration News*, 8/9, September 2001).

Japan maintains a highly restrictive migration policy based on three fundamental tenets: (a) the admission of foreign workers, on whatever basis, should be allowed only as a last resort, (b) no unskilled workers should be admitted and (c) all foreigners should be admitted only on a temporary basis (Wongboonsin, 2001b). Such policy restrictions exist despite the Revised Immigration Law that recently expanded the coverage of visa categories from 17 to 27 highly skilled occupations to reflect the diversification of purposes for landing and residence.

An explanation for the presence of unskilled foreign workers in Japan is not that they are abusing the Government's control, but that the Government turns a blind eye to their presence. In addition, the Government has relied on the "trainee" system and the importation of Japanese descendants from Latin American countries as alternatives to a foreign workforce. The latter strategy represents a unique feature of the Japanese migration policies to address the problem of local shortages. The Japanese migration law allows those Japanese descendants to enter the country under the status of long-term residents rather than foreign workers. Accordingly, they are not subject to the rules and regulations governing foreign workers, and are able to work without restrictions on their activities (Wongboonsin, 2001b). Japan has adopted the strategy of encouraging relocation of industries to overseas production sites in order to overcome the problem of local shortages.

Compared with other receiving countries in the ESCAP region, Japan is unique in terms of its attempt to identify and to exclude potential visa overstayers, as well as to encourage those in Japan to identify themselves to officials. Since 1992, the Justice Ministry has given local officials the power to grant special residency to some overstayers. Japan applies a tight border and residence control policy against undocumented immigrants. Beginning on 18 February 2000, undocumented foreigners apprehended in Japan can be subject to a five-year ban, rather than a one-year ban as was previously the case. Under the new law, they are also subject to a fine of 300,000 yen (US$ 1 = approximately 120 yen) and/or imprisonment for up to three years. Previously, only those foreigners who stayed on after their visas expired were subject to such penalties (*Migration News*, March 2000). The Justice Ministry has also announced a plan to increase the number of immigration officials by 1,100 over a five-year period in order to deal with the increase in foreign arrivals and illegal immigration (*Migration News*, August 2001).

While the Republic of Korea is not a party to the aforementioned 1951 Convention, Japan is a party; however, Japan recently adopted a policy of scaling down the influx of refugees and asylum seekers.

A different approach to a restrictive migration policy has been adopted in Hong Kong, China; and Taiwan Province of China. Despite a laissez-faire policy towards emigration, Hong Kong, China has adopted a restrictive workforce import policy. Hong Kong, China has distinct immigration policies for migrants from mainland China and from other countries. For the latter, there are import schemes that allow employers to apply for permits to bring in technicians, craftsmen and experienced operators (AMPRN, 1998). In contrast to Singapore, a strict quota system is applied to migrants who work as professionals and senior managers in the private sector as well as senior staff in the civil service and public organizations. On the other hand, foreign domestic workers are not subject to such quota restrictions. Strict control over undocumented immigration has been maintained with a strict policy of immediate repatriation of all undocumented immigrants from all countries. Tighter control is adopted against undocumented migrants from mainland China. According to a bilateral agreement with China, migrants from the mainland are subject to a daily quota determined by the Chinese Government. However, dependents of Hong Kong, China residents living in the mainland have been provided with a legal right under the Basic Law to live in Hong Kong, China. The recruitment of professionals from China is being conducted since 1994 on a trial basis.

Taiwan Province of China officially began its policy to import foreign workers in 1989, with the Employment Service Act of 1992 being the major legal basis for the import of such workers. From the beginning, it has carefully planned and controlled the flow of migrant workers at all levels, despite the fact that the legal framework of its migrant workers policy has changed several times since 1992. In contrast to Japan, Taiwan Province of China has used its migration policies as economic tools to defend its integrity by supporting indigenous businesses that operate within its borders (Tseng, 2001). By allegedly responding to a shortage of low-end workers, Taiwan Province of China has used such a policy to prevent off-shore relocation of Taiwanese companies. Taiwan Province of China has a policy to maintain domestic investment to keep up economic growth. Under the threat of relocation, permits to recruit foreign workers are not limited to sunset industries but also to high-tech ones.

As in Japan, Malaysia, New Zealand and Singapore, immigration policy in Taiwan Province of China is based on a careful selection of foreign workers from a limited number of countries. Sources include specific South-East Asian and Central American countries. This reflects the fact that foreign workers can be recruited only from countries that have extended political support to Taiwan Province of China and have signed with it a special bilateral agreement. Such a strategy is an important aspect for an economy sensitive to international isolation.

A special feature of the migration policy of Taiwan Province of China until recently was a closed-door policy towards mainland Chinese workers, despite the fact that this society shares the concern of Japan and the Republic of Korea regarding the preservation of ethnic coherence as the basis of its migration policy. Taiwan Province of China maintains that recruitment of foreign workers is of a temporary nature. Its unique rotation system of foreign recruitment complements such a policy. The system aims at maximizing economic benefits while keeping social costs to a minimum. Another important feature of its migration policy before the turn of the century was the lack of a system of permanent foreign residency. A policy shift occurred in mid-2000, when Taiwan Province of China planned to issue permanent residence permits to some of the 46,000 resident aliens who had lived on the island continuously for seven years (*Migration News*, June 2000).

Like other industrialized economies in the region, Taiwan Province of China has adopted a policy of greater openness to professionals and highly skilled foreign workers. This policy is aimed at meeting the challenges of a competitive world economy in the era of globalization (Lee, 1998). Recently, it announced a plan to issue multiple-entry visas and to extend work permits from three to six years for Chinese high-tech professionals in order to lure more talent from the mainland (*Migration News*, October 2001). Finally, Taiwan Province of China has adopted a policy to regularize and legalize the employment of unskilled migrant workers. It has offered an amnesty programme to undocumented migrant workers, mainly in the construction, manufacturing and service sectors.

## South Asia

South Asian countries are both sending and receiving countries for migrants (both forced and voluntary). After their political independence they had to deal with the problem of undocumented migrants and stateless people. As is the case in other developing countries, most South Asian countries have no policy to import foreign workers but maintain discretion over immigration control.

None of the South Asian countries has developed a national law on refugees or ratified the aforementioned Convention. However, the South Asian subregion has been host to the fourth largest concentration of refugees in the world. For example, there are Afghans from Afghanistan in Pakistan, Rohingyas (Muslims) from Myanmar in Bangladesh, Tamils from Sri Lanka in India, and Lhotsampas (Bhutanese of Nepali origin) from Bhutan in Nepal. None of the South Asian countries has a clear policy mechanism to separate forced migrants from job seekers. Refugees and stateless people are treated as illegal immigrants rather than as refugees fleeing persecution. Policies to allow non-citizens to enter the country vary among groups of migrants, with the degree of policy softness depending on kinship, religious linkages and inter-State relations. The refugee management process varies among countries in the subregion (Siwakoti, 2000; Chari, 2000; Visaria, 1999; Phryo and Bose, 1998). As in other countries in the subregion, India has adopted ad hoc policies on refugees. The policies change from time to time and from group to group, and between groups and individual cases. Discretionary powers are vested in the administrative authorities (Chari, 2000). In most countries of the South Asian subregion, the powers to grant "residential permits" are also relegated to administrators at the district and subdistrict levels. They may grant and revoke these certificates at their discretion (Phryo and Bose, 1998).

The presence of refugees and stateless people has recently been perceived as a threat and a burden. Most of the Governments of South Asian countries lack funds and logistical facilities. Accordingly, a general trend in this subregion is to curb the influx of asylum seekers and to repatriate them. Pakistan in late 2000 began restricting the entry of Afghans through the Khyber Pass (*Migration News*, January 2001). Security and law enforcement agencies have been instructed to repatriate new arrivals before they reach the refugee camps in Peshawar. Pakistan's Commission of Afghan Refugees claimed that the Government is not in a position to carry the burden of feeding 2 million Afghan refugees, considering that the World Food Programme had already discontinued relief aid to the refugees (*Migration News*, 15 September 2001). Recently, the Nepalese Government

85

## Table 5. Migration policies of receiving countries: South Asia, the Russian Federation and the Pacific

| Countries | Policy towards forced migration | Policy towards job-oriented migration | |
|---|---|---|---|
| | Signatory to the 1951 Convention and Its 1967 Protocol | Documented migrants | Undocumented migrants |
| South Asian countries | Most have an ad hoc policy to accept certain groups of forced migrants with kinship and religious linkages, and inter-state relations with the host country. | Most do not have a policy to import foreign labour but to maintain discretion concerning immigration control. | No clear mechanism to separate forced migrants from job seekers; they are considered as illegal immigrants. |
| Russian Federation | Yes, with a policy to scale down the burden of supporting forced migration. | Regulatory regimes are defined by a number of ad hoc presidential and governmental decrees and directives. Bilateral and multilateral agreements are made to prevent uncontrolled migration; to import foreign workers from a short-list of countries. | With institutional mechanism to prevent and to decrease number of undocumented migrants. |
| Australia | Recent policy to scale down the burden caused by forced migration. | Biased towards talented and high-end migrant workers from all sources; strict and transparent policy measures with national standard criteria and points system to control the quality of migrants; no policy to import unskilled migrant workers; recent policy to increase migrant intakes, particularly in field of information technology (IT). | Strict border and residence control. |
| New Zealand | Recent policy to scale down the burden caused by forced migration. | Recently shifted from a geographi-cally selective immigration policy to one diversifying the sources of migrants; biased towards talented and high-end migrant workers from all sources; strict policy measures with national standard criteria and passmarks announced weekly; recent policy to increase migrant intakes, particularly in IT fields, with new residence permits available to migrants working in jobs contributing to national economy in areas of labour shortages. | Strict border and residence control. |

signed an agreement with the Office of the United Nations High Commissioner for Refugees whereby newly arrived Tibetan refugees are escorted to immigration and later allowed to transit to India (*Migration News*, January 2001). However, critics think that it will take years for these asylum countries to repatriate all the refugees within their borders. For example, assuming no new inflows take place, it is expected that it will take Pakistan at least 20 years to complete the repatriation of the 2 million Afghan refugees living in the country (*Migration News*, 15 September 2001). At the same time, in certain South Asian countries, the adoption of policy measures to regularize undocumented migrants is subject to pressures from political parties searching for electoral votes (Siwakoti, 2000; Visaria, 1999) (see table 5).

## The Russian Federation

A different policy approach is seen in the Russian Federation. After the dissolution of the USSR in 1991, the Russian Federation has been faced with complex and diverse migration flows. Beside a large flow of refugees and forced migration from areas of ethnic and civil conflict, there has been post-empire repatriation of ethnic Russians and of other nationalities, as well as a new flow of undocumented transit or permanent immigrants from Asia and Africa. With the realization that the Russian Federation had been without legislative and institutional experience to deal with this relevant phenomenon, the State migration policy was adopted in 1994 as the first high-level policy document of the Russian Federation to deal with migration under the general programme of policies and reforms for the period 1995-1997. The key institutional mechanism to implement Russian migration policies is the Federal Migration Service, which is responsible for regulating migration, preventing undocumented migration and considering petitions for asylum (*Migration News*, October 1994).

The Russian Supreme Soviet ratified the adhesion of the Russian Federation to the aforementioned 1951 Convention in November 1992. The Law on Refugees and the Law on Forced Migration constitute that country's only general migration legislation. There laws were adopted in 1993 and amended in a restrictive way in 1997 and 1995 respectively. The amended version of the law on forced migration scales down the burden of the State authorities in terms of supporting forced migrants. It defines several categories of persons who cannot apply for the status of forced migrant. The new law on refugees closely resembles the restrictive laws adopted in Western Europe in the same period, but still meets the general standard of the 1951 Convention (Codagnone, 1998). The regulatory regime governing migration issues outside the scope of both laws is defined by a number of ad hoc presidential and governmental decrees and directives. As a supplementary policy measure, bilateral and multilateral agreements have been made with Latvia, Lithuania and Estonia in the Commonwealth of Independent States (CIS) to prevent uncontrolled migration by foreign citizens *(Migration News,* October 1994; Codagnone, 1998).

Faced with the problem of 1 million undocumented immigrants, the Government of the Russian Federation has of late been concerned with undocumented economic migration. The Moscow Municipal Government has endorsed an immigration control programme aimed at decreasing the number of undocumented foreign workers in the city by 20 per cent. It has also planned to form a so-called migration control inspectorate as a new federal body with unlimited power to detain, punish and evict undocumented immigrants. Realizing the inadequacy of migration controls, which are currently implemented only at border-crossing points, the Minister for Federal Affairs has proposed stricter migration controls and has set up a network of migration inspectorates. This does not imply that Russian policy curbs all immigration. To alleviate the negative effects of a depressed demographic situation, the Russian Federation has adopted a selective approach to the import of foreign workers from certain countries, particularly the CIS and Baltic countries, to bring in between 700,000 and 1 million foreign workers a year. A series of bilateral agreements has been concluded with those countries (Ministry of Interior, 6 July 1999; Zamuruyeva, 2001; *Pravda,* 24 July 2001).

### Pacific island countries

Australia and New Zealand have remained two major immigration countries in the Pacific. Since the early 1970s, Australia has shifted from its selective immigration policy towards a policy that emphasizes human capital from all sources. To ensure the quality of imported human capital, the Government has relied upon its Immigration Act to regulate the entry and employment of different categories of foreign nationals.

So far, Australia has maintained four categories in its migration schemes: (a) the Family Migration Programme, (b) the Economic Migration Programme, (c) the Refugee and Humanitarian Programme and (d) Special Eligibility. The Family Migration Programme allows Australian citizens, permanent residents and eligible New Zealand citizens to sponsor some of their relatives who are living overseas to migrate to Australia. The Refugee and Humanitarian Programme is provided to express Australia's commitment to the aforementioned 1951 Convention; however,

Australia has recently scaled down the influx of these migrants (*Migration News,* September 2001). The Special Eligibility programme applies to former citizens, former residents, New Zealand citizens, families of New Zealand citizens, and permanent residents of Norfolk Island.

The Australian policy towards economic migrants can be considered biased towards the highly skilled who can contribute to Australia's economic performance. As in certain receiving countries in other subregions, Australia has a long-standing tradition of not permitting entry to unskilled foreign workers.

Authorization to work in Australia can be categorized mainly according to the length of the work period: (a) permanent or on a long-term basis and (b) temporary. The former, under the so-called "economic migration programme," is restricted to foreign workers with skills and talents that would benefit the Australian economy. The latter applies to "temporary workers" and refers to skilled migrants who work in Australia at pre-arranged jobs for temporary periods, as well as to expatriates sent by their overseas employers to work in Australia. Unlike most receiving countries in other subregions, Australia increased its immigration intake by 15,000 in 2000/01. This includes foreign professionals with training in information technology, nursing and accounting; employment in regional areas and under employer-nominated schemes; and those prepared to pay a social security bond of A$ 10,000 (US$ 1 = A$ 1.56), with an extra A$ 4,000 for each parent sponsored.

New Zealand has until now adopted a geographically selective approach to its immigration policy. In the 1970s, the focus was on a narrow range of traditional source countries in Europe, particularly, Ireland and the United Kingdom of Great Britain and Northern Ireland. From the mid-1980s to the late 1990s, New Zealand welcomed migrant workers from the South Pacific, professionally qualified South Africans, and migrants from East Asia with financial resources and business skills. Currently, the government policy is to diversify the sources of migration to New Zealand. This is particularly the case for migrants in the general category, focusing on young skilled migrants intending to work in New Zealand. The government policy is to deliver a "global immigration target" from year to year. Other migration categories in New Zealand include the business investment category, general category, family policy and humanitarian policy. While the Australian point system is a major mechanism to control the quality of migrants, New Zealand has relied on the so-called "passmark", announced on a weekly basis, to reach its objectives (New Zealand Immigration Information, 2001). Recently, New Zealand's Ministry of Immigration presented a proposal to allow thousands of foreigners with short-term work permits to eventually obtain permanent residence. According to the proposal, the new residence permits will be available only to those working in jobs contributing to New Zealand's economic development in areas with shortages (*Migration News,* September 2001).

# CONCLUSION

The Governments of both sending and receiving countries in the ESCAP region have recently reconsidered their migration policies. This study has found that the migration policies of both sending and receiving countries in the ESCAP region have reflected an increased governmental sensitivity to socio-economic and political pressures at home on one hand, and the impact of the globalized knowledge economy on the other. On the demand side, the general trend is that receiving countries are moving towards decreasing dependence on cheap and low-end foreign workers, despite an awareness of the structural need for them. Among the countries examined in this paper, the Republic of Korea serves as an exceptional case in realizing the structural demand for cheap and low-end foreign workers, and moving towards the institutionalization of an immigration system. At the same time, certain countries have adopted policies selectively to open their doors to migrants from countries with a cultural similarity to local populations and/or with political-economic ties. Bilateral service agreements between receiving and sending countries are more and more being resorted to as extra policy measures to minimize risks while maximizing national economic growth. There is a very close linkage between the countries' migration policies and their diplomatic policies, particularly those with restrictive migration policies. To minimize dependence on low-end migrant workers, certain Asian receiving countries have adopted a strategy of moving towards a knowledge economy. The case is particularly clear in Malaysia and Singapore. The migration policies of most receiving countries with developed and newly industrializing economies in both Asia and the Pacific have lately been and will continue to be biased towards talented and high-end migrants (both transient and permanent settlers) worldwide. Accordingly, migration policies in the region can be expected to move increasingly towards a double standard. This study has found that, despite similar concerns and policy objectives, policy measures and migration management processes vary widely among the countries investigated.

On the supply side, sending countries can be categorized into those with explicit policies to encourage emigration and those without policies to export their workforce. It is clear that the recent financial crisis has prompted Asian countries with export policies to step up not only emigration but also the protection of their overseas workforce. At the turn of the century, many of them have prioritized and/ or minimized restrictions on the export of knowledgeable and skilled migrant workers so as to maintain their competitiveness in the world market in this era of a globalized knowledge economy. The case is clearer in Asia than it is in the Pacific. The study has also found that in most Asian sending countries Governments are playing a more active role in managing the flows of emigration. Asian countries with an explicit policy to encourage emigration are particularly aware of the benefits of emigration in solving domestic unemployment problems and in producing sources of foreign exchange and remittances. As in the case of receiving countries, policy measures vary among the sending countries examined in this study.

The study also found that the issue of undocumented migration has become a major concern to Governments of both receiving and sending countries in the region. While receiving countries have tightened their border controls, sending countries have managed to regulate emigration with stiff penalties for errant migrants. The case is particularly clear in China. While most receiving countries have a policy to crack down on undocumented migration and unauthorized employment, the issue of overstayers has received little attention. A growing trend in receiving countries is the emergence of policy measures to punish persons involved in human trafficking and in the employment of undocumented migrant workers. Another trend involves changing attitudes towards recognizing undocumented migrants as human beings. This can be seen in the recent initiative of countries such as the Republic of Korea and Thailand, which include such migrants under the coverage of welfare provisions. At the same time, the attitude of receiving countries towards forced migration remains mixed.

Overall, Governments of countries and areas in the ESCAP region maintain their sovereignty to manage the flows of migration (both forced and voluntary) unilaterally. Bilateral cooperation between receiving and sending countries and areas serves only as an extra measure in their migration policies.

It is doubtful that certain aspects of the current migration policies of both receiving and sending countries will result in an orderly migration flow and will allow migration to contribute to national development. This is particularly the case with those policies prioritizing high-end migrant workers and minimizing low-end ones. A clear example is the case of the Philippines, where there has been long-term economic stagnation despite the export of skilled and high-end migrant workers. Besides, the recent Indonesian policy to prioritize high-end migrant workers and to minimize unskilled migration can be expected to aggravate the problem of undocumented migration.

Accordingly, upgrading the skills of migrants as human resources in both sending and receiving countries should be considered an important measure to complement such migration policies. It is also necessary that sending countries develop a policy regime to make sure that remittances are appropriately invested for long-term development at the individual, family, community and national levels. Sending countries encourage temporary labour emigration rather than emigration to settle overseas. They encourage not only the host countries in transferring technology and know-how to migrant workers but also the migrant workers in using their experience to contribute to the economy upon return to their homeland. Otherwise, the problem of brain drain could delay the economic development of certain sending countries.

At the same time, it is necessary for receiving countries to ensure that job-oriented immigration contributes to national economic development. In all the countries examined in this study, there are regulatory regimes requiring that firms employ migrant workers because they cannot find suitably qualified workers in the local workforce, rather than because of their desire for cheap workers. However, unauthorized employment in many countries, particularly in Asia, reveals the problems of law enforcement. In addition, labour market tests are needed in a number of the Asian countries investigated in this study. The case of Australia is clear in terms of assuring that immigration contributes to national economic development. Key explanations are that migration policy is considered an integral part of Australian economic and social development policy, and that the policy is supported by strict and transparent policy measures governing migrant workers, employers and other people involved in migration and recruitment processes.

In terms of forced migration, the poorer Asian countries are bearing a disproportionate burden of humanitarian relief. Meanwhile, developed countries are curbing the influx of refugees despite being parties to the aforementioned 1951 Convention. Thus, a sharp increase in humanitarian aid is needed. In all cases of either forced or voluntary migration, cooperation is needed not only between sending and receiving countries but also in the form of regional and multilateral cooperation. Such cooperation should be aimed not only at producing orderly migration flows, but also at reducing the development gap among countries.

# REFERENCES

Asia Pacific Migration Research Network (APMRN) (1998). *"Migration Issues in the Asia Pacific"*, various issues.

Baharon bin Talib (1998). "Migration country paper: Policy aspects", paper presented at the Regional Workshop on Transnational Migration and Development in ASEAN Countries, 25-27 May, Bangkok.

Chari, P.R. (2000). "The refugees situation in South Asia and its security implications", *Report on the IPCS Seminar,* (New Delhi, Institute of Peace and Conflict Studies), 26 November.

Codagnone, Cristiano (1998). *New Migration and Migration Policies in Post-Soviet Russia,* Working Paper No. 2, (Rome, Ethnobarometer Programme).

Dang, Nguyen Anh (1998). "Vietnam country paper: Academic aspects", paper presented at the Regional Workshop on Transnational Migration and Development in ASEAN Countries, 25-27 May, Bangkok.

Htay, Maung (1998). "Policy toward immigration and emigration in Myanmar and the possibility of linking migration policy with trade policy (draft)", paper presented to the Regional Workshop on Transnational Migration and Development in ASEAN Countries, 25-27 May, Bangkok.

Hugo, Graeme (1998). "The demographic underpinnings of current and future international migration in Asia", *Asian and Pacific Migration Journal,* vol. 7, No. 1, pp. 1-25.

Institute of Population Studies (IPS) and Institute of Asian Studies (IAS) (1997). *Human Resources Development and Migration Pattern among ASEAN Member Countries,* Working Paper for the Ad-hoc Committee on Human Resources Development, (Bangkok, IPS and IAS).

Lee, Joseph S. (1998). "The impact of the Asian financial crisis on foreign workers in Taiwan", *Asian and Pacific Migration Journal,* vol. 7, Nos. 3-4, pp. 137-143.

*Migration News* (Geneva), various issues from January 1990 to September 2001.

Ministry of the Interior, Russian Federation (1999). "Illegal migration in Russia and EU member States is to a large extent organized by organised criminal groups", 6 July, (press release).

Myint, Nyan (1998). "Myanmar country paper: Academic aspects", paper presented at the Regional Workshop on Transnational Migration and Development in ASEAN Countries, 25-27 May, Bangkok.

Pachusanond, Chumporn (2001). "Regulatory regimes governing foreign workers in Thailand", paper presented to the Ministry of Labour and Social Welfare, Bangkok.

Phyro, Aung and Tapan Bose (1998). "Refugees in South Asia: An overview", *Refugee Watch,* No. 1, January.

*Pravda* (2001). "Ministry for Federal Affairs proposes migration inspectorates", *Pravda,* 24 July.

Premi, Mahendra K. and M.D. Mathur (1995). "Emigration dynamics: The Indian context", *International Migration,* vol. 33, Nos. 3, 4.

Scalabrini Migration Center (SMC) (2000). *Philippines – Migration in 2000,* (Quezon City, Philippines, SMC).

Shah, Nasra M. (1995). "Emigration dynamics from and within South Asia", *International Migration,* vol. 33, Nos. 3, 4.

Siwakoti, Gopal Krishna (2000). "Statistics of refugee influx in South Asia: Developing a more global regime", *INHURED International.*

Tirtosudarmo, Riwanto (1998). "Indonesian country paper: Academic aspects", paper presented at the Regional Workshop on Transnational Migration and Development in ASEAN Countries, 25-27 May, Bangkok.

Tjiptoherijanto, Prijono (1998). "Indonesian Government perception on international migration and its policies", paper presented at the Regional Workshop on Transnational Migration and Development in ASEAN Countries, 25-27 May, Bangkok.

Tsay, Ching-Lung and Ji-Ping Lin (2000). "Working and living conditions of Thai contract workers in Taiwan: A study on individual outcomes of migration", paper presented at the National Seminar of the Research Project on Thai Migrant Workers in South-East and East Asia, 18 September, Bangkok.

Tseng, Yen-Feng (2001). "The State and the foreigners: Foreign workers policies in Taiwan", paper presented at a meeting of the International Sociological Association RC 31 Research Committee on the Sociology of Migration, Migration Between States and Markets, 17-19 May, University of Liege, Belgium.

United Nations (1996). *World Population Monitoring 1993, with a Special Report on Refugees,* (United Nations publication, Sales No. E.95.XIII.8).

United Nations (1998a). *International Migration Policies,* (United Nations publication, Sales No. E.98.XIII.8).

United Nations (1998b). *World Population Monitoring 1997: International Migration and Development,* (United Nations publication, Sales No. E.98.XIII.4).

Visaria, Pravin M. (1999). "Statement delivered at the 32nd Session of the Commission on Population and Development on Population Growth, Structure and Distribution", 22-30 March, United Nations, New York.

Wongboonsin, Patcharawalai (2000). "Impact of economic crisis on migration policies in the ASEAN region", *Journal of Demography,* vol. 16, No. 1 (March).

Wongboonsin, Patcharawalai (2001a). "Regulatory regimes governing foreign workers in Malaysia, the Philippines, Singapore, and Australia", research report presented to the Ministry of Labour and Social Welfare, Bangkok (unpublished).

Wongboonsin, Patcharawalai (2001b). "Transnational migration policies of ASEAN and non-ASEAN countries", paper presented at the Seminar on International Studies, Kyushu University, 5 August (unpublished).

Yap, Mui Teng (1998). "Singapore country paper: Policy aspects", paper presented at the Regional Workshop on Transnational Migration and Development in ASEAN Countries, 25-27 May, Bangkok.

Zamuruyeva, Inga (2001). "New Inspectorate to Clamp Down on Illegal Immigration", *Gazeta.Ru,* 18 July.